business *masterminds*

jack
WELCH

ROBERT HELLER

A Dorling Kindersley Book

LONDON, NEW YORK, SYDNEY, DELHI, PARIS,
MUNICH, and JOHANNESBURG

Senior Editor Adèle Hayward
Senior Art Editor Caroline Marklew
DTP Designer Jason Little
Production Controller Sarah Coltman
Senior Managing Editor Stephanie Jackson
Managing Art Editor Nigel Duffield

Produced for Dorling Kindersley by
Grant Laing Partnership
48 Brockwell Park Gardens,
London SE24 9BJ
Managing Editor Jane Laing
Project Editor Frank Ritter
Project Art Editor Steve Wilson

First American Edition, 2001
00 01 02 03 04 05 10 9 8 7 6 5 4 3 2 1

Published in the United States by
Dorling Kindersley Publishing, Inc.
95 Madison Avenue
New York, New York 10016

Library of Congress Cataloging-in-Publication Data

Heller, Robert, 1932-
  Jack Welch / Robert Heller.
    p. cm.
  Includes index.
  ISBN 0-7894-7159-0 (alk. paper)
  1. Welch, Jack (John Francis), 1935- 2. Chief
executive officers–United States–Biography. 3.
Industrial management–United States–Case studies.
4. Leadership–United States–Case studies. 5. Electric
industries–United States–Management–Case studies.
6. General Electric Company–Management. I. Title.
  HD9697.A3 U545 2000
  338.7'62138'092–dc21
                                      00-055503

Reproduced by Colourpath, London
Printed in Hong Kong by Wing King Tong

Author's Acknowledgments
The many sources for this book have been
acknowledged in the text, but I must now
express my great debt to everybody, above
all to the Mastermind himself. Nor would
the book exist but for the inspiration and
effort of the excellent Dorling Kindersley
team – to whom my warm thanks.

Packager's Acknowledgments
Grant Laing Partnership would like to
thank the following for their help and
participation:
Index Kay Ollerenshaw
Picture Research Andy Sansom

Picture Credits
The publisher would like to thank the
following for their kind permission to
reproduce the following photographs:
Corbis UK Ltd: 100; E.O. Hoppe 29;
Robert Mass 1, 4, 91; **Courtesy of
GECrotonville:** 9, 13; **Popperfoto:**
Peter Morgan/Reuters 25; Reuters 36, 52;
Rex Features: David Lomax 77; KMLA 51;
R. Lawrence 48; **Tony Stone Images:** Eric
Sander 12; Grant Taylor 88; Jon Riley 75.

Front jacket: **Katz Features:** Delluc/XPn

See our complete catalog at
www.dk.com

Contents

The corporate pathfinder

Jack Welch was the quintessential corporate manager of the late 20th century. Retiring as CEO of General Electric (GE) in 2000, he remains the ultimate role model. His fame is based partly on the astounding wealth he has created. On April Fool's Day 1981, when Welch took over, the stock market valued GE at $13.9 billion. In the fall of 1999 that value had swollen nearly 30 times to $410.8 billion.

This stunning success helped persuade corporate America (and then the world) that enriching shareholders was the right objective for CEOs, and eminently practicable – especially if they followed Welch's methods. Many adopted Welch practices, such as "restructuring" to streamline costs, concentrating on core businesses with leadership positions, and forcing responsibility down to subordinates.

But their hero was a moving target. As CEO, Welch restlessly searched for new initiatives that would sustain and enhance GE's progress. He has said, "To be vital, an organization has to repeat itself, start again, get new ideas, renew itself." He has proved that companies – even giants – can be vitally renewed by management of driving will.

Robert Heller

Biography

John Francis Welch, Jr., was born in 1936 in Massachusetts. His father, a railroad conductor, and mother were both in their forties at the time, and had no other children. The young Jack was devoted above all to his mother, Grace, who taught him the importance of controlling one's own destiny and of bluntly confronting reality. Blessed with Irish blood, charm, and high intelligence, Welch was the first member of his family to go to college. He studied chemical engineering at the University of Massachusetts, going on to earn a Ph.D. at the University of Illinois.

Neither university was fashionable: despite his intellect, Welch had failed to win an Ivy League scholarship. This failure, and his relative poverty, only reinforced his drive to succeed. This driving ambition was obvious from the moment he arrived in Pittsfield, Massachusetts in 1960 to take his first job, working in General Electric's plastics business. It was not a typical GE company: dominated by electrical products ranging from vast turbogenerators to domestic appliances and light bulbs, GE had strayed unprofitably into plastics via research into industrial resins.

Outstanding performance

After being dissuaded from leaving by his boss and mentor, Reuben Gutoff, Welch found this small and far from lucrative operation of 300 employees ideal for developing and displaying the "turnaround" talents that were later applied so successfully to the entire giant company. Rising rapidly, he became general manager in

1968, taking sales to $2 billion. Wherever he went, and whatever he did, Welch proved himself highly competent – and highly ambitious. In 1973 he had risen to divisional vice-president, looking after the consumer products and services businesses. There his performance won this glowing tribute from Gutoff:

"Overall Jack's 1972 performance was outstanding [underlined]. He managed a portfolio of diverse businesses to achieve exceptional short-term profit results while simultaneously investing aggressively for future growth... technically very strong, has entrepreneurial drive, is bright & quick. Sets high standards for himself and demands same of people who work for him. Extremely imaginative and creative. Likes to operate 'outside the dots,' but at the same time is very 'maze bright.' Jack is profit & results oriented – disdains diversions that detract from business accomplishments. Has great marketing skills. Strong leader."

Nor was that all. The boss discerned "Another key result: Clearly developed a runner-up for his job in event of promotion." The divisional vice-president himself had no doubt where that possible promotion should lead. That 1973 Evaluation and Development Summary states firmly that his "longer-range" intention was to be "Chief Executive Officer of General Electric Company." Eight years later, aged 45, he had the job, and proceeded to turn the company upside down – even though GE had just been voted the best-managed company among the *Fortune* 500 (the biggest US industrial and commercial groups).

For good measure, Welch's predecessor, Reg Jones, had been hailed as the best CEO among the 500. The new appointee would dismantle much of Jones' legacy; but the most important part of that inheritance was GE's tradition of periodically branching out in new directions under a new, internally appointed CEO. Jones did not (like all too many departing CEOs) want a successor who would preserve the status quo. On the contrary, Jones felt that the culture had become constipated and that bureaucracy was rampant. According to an article in *Fortune* magazine by Thomas F. O'Boyle, "Welch's tendency to rattle cages and shake things up was exactly what Jones wanted."

The cage-rattler's appointment was a triumph of succession planning, which had long been a GE strength. There was plenty of competition for the top job, although Welch, despite (or because of) those maverick ways, was plainly a very strong candidate. In 1977 he moved (against his will, but at Jones's insistence) to Fairfield, Connecticut, where GE has its headquarters, becoming vice-chairman and executive officer in 1979. He had added to his plastics laurels by recording successes in medical diagnostics (another turnaround) and in GE's financial business. This grew out of supplying credit for purchases of GE equipment and, as GE Capital, was to be a sustaining, superb engine of growth during Welch's reign.

Blitzkrieg aggressiveness

Achieving that growth has been the dominant theme of Welch's career since he won the crown – a promotion announced in December 1980. For all the successes of Welch and other GE managers over the previous decade, the company's performance was far worse than the *Fortune* 500 accolades indicated. Adjusted for inflation, the share price had halved. Welch made it his mission to reverse this decline in value, and to do so in spectacular fashion: he wanted to make GE the world's most valuable company – in the late 1990s, it vied with Microsoft for that distinction. That meant removing all the obstacles to profitable growth, and doing so forcibly.

When *Fortune* named Welch as "Manager of the Century" in 1999, the citation noted that the new CEO had "proposed to blow up [GE's] portfolio of businesses, its bureaucracy, many of its practices and traditions, its very culture." True to form, Welch not only proposed – he disposed, acting "with what seemed at the time like blitzkrieg aggressiveness." But in retrospect, Welch believed he had moved too slowly.

He founded his blitzkrieg on a simple proposition. GE's businesses had to be first or second in their market, or they would be radically reformed, sold – or closed. Scores were shut. GE's workforce came down by 100,000 in a ruthless clear-out that earned Welch the nickname of "Neutron Jack," after the bomb that kills people but leaves buildings intact. The "slain" included 400 corporate planners who

Laughing with intent
Training of GE executives at Crotonville is galvanized by the searching, take-no-prisoners style of Jack Welch (right), who uses the sessions to promulgate his values companywide.

had been Jones' pride and joy: they went, along with the much-praised process they had created.

Welch preferred to run strategy through meetings, ranging from 500 top executives gathered in Florida in January (preceded by a preparatory meeting of 140) to quarterly gatherings of the 30 topmost people at the company's own business school at Croton-on-Hudson, NY. Leaders of each division got full days with the boss to review three-year strategic plans, annual budgets, and development of the managers (GE had 3,000) who were within their division.

A relentless tide of profits

As that generous allocation of his time indicates, Welch is a hands-on, confrontational, face-to-face manager who talks and talks (despite a slight stammer) and believes that "The idea flow from the human spirit is absolutely unlimited," and that "All you have to do is tap into that well." His two decades at GE have been marked by major new companywide initiatives – recently, for example, a high-powered drive for fault-free quality – which have created and been reinforced by a relentless tide of profits. Net income rose from $1.5 billion in 1981 to $8.2 billion in 1997 on a tripling of sales.

Two-fifths of those sales are accounted for by GE Capital. The tremendous success of Welch's "baby" has disguised the fact that, had GE been confined only to its industrial interests, its growth would have been far from outstanding. The gains have also been boosted by acquisitions: in Welch's first two years, GE got into 118 new businesses, joint ventures, or buys, while selling 71 old ones. The big buys since then include an unhappy venture into Wall Street and the purchase of RCA, whose NBC television channel became highly successful under GE management.

Welch's GE salaries, bonuses, and stock options have made him a billionaire. But he is by no means all work and no play. Always big on sports, he has become an avid golfer who plays with the best, such as the great golfing professional Greg Norman. Divorced and remarried, he has two children. His family has had to accommodate to a hectic schedule as Welch whirls (often literally, in a helicopter) around the GE empire. His packed schedule as both leader and educator of GE's managers means that he moves fast — sometimes too fast.

He can make judgments too quickly and on too little knowledge. He is, however, equally quick to correct his errors. He does not intellectualize about management. Rather, he has taught by example and proved theories in practice. His personal style has translated admirably into an organizationwide culture that has transcended the infamous disadvantages of size.

The question of succession

Welch has continued, as in his early career, "to achieve exceptional short-term profit results while simultaneously investing aggressively for future growth," and to insist that his executives do likewise. Other early strengths, like his farsightedness in developing his own replacement, became vital in the 1990s. In 1991, with a decade to spare, Welch said that "From now on, choosing my successor is the most important decision I'll make. It occupies a considerable amount of thought every day." That succession, and its achievements, will be the final test of a performance that has already left an indelible legacy.

1

Making managers lead

Getting into the saddle and leading from the front ● How Welch distinguishes leadership from management and turns managers into leaders ● **Mastering the seven basics for business success** ● Fighting the battle to beat bureaucracy by cutting out layers and eliminating red tape ● **Using meetings to galvanize and integrate management** ● Spreading best practice between managers and between companies ● **How to balance hands-off management and delegation with hands-on, personal leadership**

The distinction between leaders and managers, and the driving necessity to transform the latter into the former, is at the core of Jack Welch's preaching and practice. His seven-point program for management by leadership was clearly articulated, not just by his words but his actions, as he led one of the world's largest business organizations into unprecedented success:

- Develop a vision for the business.
- Change the culture to achieve the vision.
- Flatten the organization.
- Eliminate bureaucracy.
- Empower individuals.
- Raise quality.
- Eliminate boundaries.

None of these stages could occur without leadership, to which management plays a secondary, supporting role. As Welch sees it, the difference between a leader and a manager is that between a general and an officer down the line. The leader's job is to allocate the available resources of people and money rigorously so as to generate optimum results. Those results will, however, be won under the "management" of the officers.

Welch awards his generals a directive, strategic role, for which he demands exceptional qualities. "It takes courage and tough-mindedness," he says, "to pick the bets, put the resources behind them, articulate the vision to the employees, and explain why you said yes to this one and no to that one." The tactical work is left to others – and that means without interference. Even the language used is important. "Call people managers," he says, "and they are going to start managing things, getting in the way."

In the light of that forceful view, it is a supreme irony that in November 1999, *Fortune* magazine named Welch "The Greatest Manager" of the century just ended. He is, however, deliberately overstating his case. GE's managers are expected to lead at every level, not just at the top. Welch wants the people all the way down to be, like himself, hands-on executives engaged in the restless pursuit of better and better performance. He simply wants to emphasize that the job of a manager is to make dynamic choices, not to spread resources out evenly, "like butter on bread." In Welch's view, that is bureaucracy, on which he has waged unrelenting war for decades.

Controlling bureaucracy

Large corporations breed structure upon structure, layer upon layer, bureaucracy upon bureaucracy, rules upon rules. Welch, however, believes in minimalist form. As he cut layers, he doubled (if not more) the "span of control" (the number of managers reporting to a single superior). Having to handle, say, a dozen sub-managers imposed a major extra workload on business leaders. Their psychological burdens also intensified after Welch abolished the highest layer of all, the "sector heads" who shared responsibility for groups of businesses, but whose real role was vague – and harmful.

Most large organizations have these superfluous levels, which in nearly all cases slow decision-making, blur responsibility, and create undoable jobs. Welch will not tolerate any of these three defects. He decreed that heads of the businesses (themselves reorganized into coherent entities) would report directly to him. Welch's own span of control thus became a dozen on that count alone. But the burden weighed lightly on his shoulders, because the business chieftains were left (in fact, forced) to make their own decisions: in a word, to lead.

Before Welch, some 300 managers had enjoyed "P&L [profit and loss] responsibility." They had profit and revenue targets to meet and were judged on their financial results. By the time Welch finished, the numbers had been decimated: just 30 leaders were P&L-responsible. Before Welch, GE had actually pioneered the idea of dividing a company into "strategic business units," or SBUs, each with its own accounts and a responsible manager in charge.

In theory, creation of SBUs makes the unwieldy manageable, while teaching and testing many executives in exercising full business responsibility. The system's virtues, however, are offset by vices: managers often will not cooperate with other businesses and will do all they can (sensibly or not) to protect their short-term profits – which, of course, have to be examined continually by central financial monitors. At General Electric, control had become the be-all and end-all under the reign of the company's bureaucracy.

Sharing information

Welch showed that the systems beloved by bureaucrats can be turned into dynamic forces by dynamic leadership. As a supreme example, Welch uses meetings and committees, not as controls, but as his most powerful management tool. The critical sessions are those of the Corporate Executive Council. The CEC meets once a quarter at the company's in-house business school, Crotonville, at Croton-on-Hudson, NY. Attended by 30 of the leading executives of the corporation, these sessions are described as "food fights." Welch uses them to check on progress, to display leadership (his own) and encourage it in others, and to exchange ideas and information:

"The enormous benefit we get from our meetings is that we end up being smarter than anybody else. It's not that we have a higher I.Q. But after two days with the CEC, having to talk about everything from TV networks to the Indonesian economy just to understand our own businesses, we can walk out and talk to anybody at a cocktail party, and be the smartest guys in town. And we may not be as smart as most of the other people there – it's just that we're exposed to so much more information."

The CEC sessions also subject the organization's leaders to challenges and tests; share the lessons of success and failure; and transfer new ideas, derived from different businesses, from one to the others. Sharing is also vital to the Boca Raton meeting in January, when 500 executives troop down to Florida to discuss the year ahead. The lucky ones get the chance to present their achievements in front of their peers. That meant 29 of the 500 in 1998. Welch takes notes (a constant habit) as they talk, in part preparing for a final wind-up speech that pulls no punches.

Welch does not believe that leaders should peddle comfort. Their role is to rock the boat, to urge people forward by forcible, even excessive language. The magazine *Business Week* reported this wind-up in 1998:

"The one unacceptable comment from a GE leader in '98 will be 'Prices are lower than we thought, and we couldn't get costs out fast enough to make our commitments'. Unacceptable! Unacceptable behavior, because prices will be lower than you're planning, so you better start taking action this week."

The whole Welch message is recorded on video and sent immediately to the 500 executives' desks, complete with instructions on its use with their own people. In 1998 that meant 750 videos in eight languages, including Mandarin and Hungarian. By the end of January, some two-thirds of GE's workforce had seen the tape.

Pursuing best practice

The CEC and Boca Raton meetings are weapons in the war for "best practice," which plays a key part in Welch's management philosophy. If every part of an organization uses the best ideas and methods discovered anywhere else, the whole group's performance will be optimized. For example, a stellar performance in industrial diamonds (in four years, a fourfold rise in return on investment, and a halving in costs) attracted hundreds of other GE managers. They were understandably eager to discover how the diamond plant had raised efficiency so much that no investment in plant and machinery would be required for another 10 years.

Welch uses the regular meetings to publicize such achievements and the methodology behind them. But the decision to adopt a given best practice is left (following Welch's basic principle) to the individual businesses and

"**We are out to get a feeling and a spirit of total openness. That's alien to a manager of 25 or 30 years ago who got ahead by knowing a little more than the employee who works for him [or her].**"
Jack Welch Speaks (1998)

their leaders. Welch loves new ideas, and insists that they get a full airing. He will act as hot gospeler for the ideas he likes. But he does not believe in telling general managers how to run their companies. That is their job alone.

Delegating responsibility

Welch's leadership theory obviously depends heavily on the power of delegation. That is needed in all organizations and depends in turn on the excellence of selection. "People say people are important in every business," he notes. But their importance and that of delegation are magnified by the very nature of GE. In a multibusiness company, the CEO's knowledge of those businesses is far less than that of somebody running a concentrated company like Coca-Cola. Welch has to have "real experts and real good people" to run his businesses: "If I don't have them, the game's over."

But the leader cannot simply hand over all power to good people and then abdicate his authority. Welch neatly balances hands-off management – giving his business heads full autonomy and the power of decision – with hands-on leadership. In addition to his major corporate activities, Welch directly intervenes in lesser matters, such as:

- ▨ The launch of a joint venture cable TV program by the NBC broadcasting company and its partner, Dow Jones.
- ▨ The decision to enter pet insurance in the UK.
- ▨ The flat rejection of an advertising campaign. ("I like advertising. I like promotion. I'm the advertising manager of our company. I love it.")
- ▨ The upgrading of the comparatively poor performance of tubes used in GE's X-ray and CT-scan machines.

The unpredictability of Welch's interventions itself acts as a powerful stimulus to the managers on whom he might pounce. Welch can afford the time for this detailed intervention because the quarterly and annual results seldom bring any surprises. He monitors performance against exact and exacting performance targets. His "direct reports," and especially the dozen operating heads of GE businesses, exercise the same control over their subordinates. Welch's personal forays, however, add ginger to what might otherwise degenerate into an arid, figure-bound system. "Gingering up" is the essence of his leadership style, which is fundamentally confrontational.

Exceeding commitments

Intense internal competition makes such confrontation a fundamental aspect of life at GE. Welch's style guarantees that his managers go into his one-to-one meetings "psyched up," or, as one of them puts it, "ready for combat." Pulling punches is not allowed here, either: so, says the same man, "You'd better have a thick skin, or when you come out you will be a hurting person." The hurt is also felt in larger gatherings, especially by anybody running a low-performing business. According to a former GE executive, "When somebody is floundering, there is a little bit of... shunning; the guy's not so popular at the coffee breaks."

Those who flounder cannot complain: they know what is expected. Welch leads by having goals for all important measures – productivity, inventory turns, quality, working capital, customer satisfaction, and so on. The goals are clearly set out and treated as rock-solid "commitments." At the quarterly meetings, the competition sets in as every combatant seeks to come out top in exceeding commitments. This law of the jungle suits Welch well. He believes in the survival of the fittest and applies that law to all businesses within GE, to GE itself, and to all executives, not just those at the top.

Winning hearts and minds

At a time when middle managers were widely seen as a desperately endangered species, Welch saw their liberation and empowerment as the key to productivity gains, without which GE could not achieve his goal of significantly outgrowing the US economy. Getting the 2,000 top executives to share his ideas was not even half the battle, even though that fight alone took eight years and massive removals, replacements, and reshuffles. Another 100,000 lower managers still had to be reached. Welch's recipe for winning their hearts and minds – and, of course, their effort – had four parts:

- Free managers to manage – and to rise.
- Defeat bureaucracy and rigidity.
- Generate and use new ideas.
- Empower workers to flourish and grow.

It is not enough to preach these principles. How you practice them is vital. Welch believes that leadership must be personalized. So nobody at GE, even the topmost executives, gets a formal letter from the CEO. His message may well be blunt, but it comes in his own neat handwriting. Nor are salaries, bonus payments, and stock options dished out automatically to the two dozen people who report to him directly. Rewards are always accompanied by frank, face-to-face evaluation.

Rewards for these top executives, like those all the way down, are large, depending on the achievement: bonus payments can quadruple from one year to the next, and reach as much as 70 percent of base pay. Within an overall target of, say, 4 percent more on the salary bill, somebody exceptional may pocket a 25 percent raise without promotion. Welch also spreads stock options far more widely than in the past; a third of his professional employees have become eligible. Options have created over 1,200 GE millionaires; the CEO himself is a billionaire.

As run by Welch, the rewards and options differentiate sharply between one manager and another, one year and the next, one business and another. "I can't stand non-differentiated stuff," he has said. "We live in differentiation. You can't run these 12 businesses as if they were one institution." It is like working for a hard-nosed, demanding, but generous entrepreneur – a description that fits Welch to a T, and which he thinks should describe the behavior of all leaders.

Knowing the people

Welch believes in appointing business heads whose approach is compatible with his entrepreneurial thrust, and who can be trusted to run their operations without interference from above. His greatest pride lies in his ability to find and nurture highly able managers. This is not a matter of hunch, but of hard, organized work. On his reckoning, half of his time goes on people issues – and on getting to know people. A cardinal Welch principle is that the leader should really know the top people in the organization – their faces, their names, what they do, their key abilities, and how they manage.

One writer found that Welch personally knew at least a thousand of his managerial subordinates. When a job needs filling, Welch already knows the candidates, and will pick or endorse the person he considers best for the job, regardless of seniority or rank – or how many others are leapfrogged in the process. The main mechanisms involved, again, are meetings. So-called "Session C" reviews run from April through May and cover all the businesses and 3,000 executives, with special emphasis on the top 500.

A team of four led by Welch may work from 8.00 a.m. to 1.00 p.m. at the headquarters of the business with its CEO and his human resources head. Welch comes armed with a full briefing on every person to be discussed. He knows how they themselves assess their strengths and weaknesses, what development they are thought to require, what their goals are, and what their bosses think about these same issues. Even lunch on these packed days is concentrated work. Welch makes a point of lunching with women and minority managers as part of his effort to increase their presence in GE's senior ranks. (They are still not strongly represented, but Welch does at least try.)

Session C meetings are typically confrontational. Throughout the day, Welch challenges the business leaders to defend their plans for promotions, succession, and postings. In the end, the leaders get who they want, but they have to convince Welch that they, like him, are on the hunt for people who clearly possess what he describes as "E to the fourth power." "E" stands for:

- Energy
- Energizing others
- competitive Edge
- Execution

The subordinate bosses are put through a stiff test of their own leadership qualities at the C sessions. Stiff testing is a key characteristic of Welch's leadership style; but are the tests, as some critics have argued, too stiff?

Toughing it

In his early years, Welch became the unwilling exemplar for a mode of management that was quite contrary to his true ideal. In 1984, *Fortune* magazine named him as the toughest of America's tough bosses, a man who made people tremble by his aggression in meetings; who attacked others, "criticizing, demeaning, ridiculing, humiliating"; who you contradicted at your intellectual peril. Welch hated this "toughest boss" accolade and has never received it again. He is certainly tough, and, as noted, is nothing if not confrontational. But he can be outargued, and he is both human and humane. As one executive told Noel M. Tichy (the academic and consultant who revitalized GE's Crotonville academy for Welch):

> "...if you're confident about what you're doing, and willing to stand up for what you believe, you're probably going to be OK...If he ever catches you 'winging it' [improvising on inadequate preparation] you're in trouble. Real trouble. You have to go in with in-depth information."

That toughness is an essential element in the leadership that Welch practices and admires. It is applied without fear and favor to both insiders and to executives imported as a result of GE's innumerable takeovers. When RCA was acquired, for a then-record $6.5 billion, Welch examined the management of its best-known business, the NBC broadcasting network, the largest in the land, and found it wanting. Managers were mired in the past and had to change. If not, Welch told 100 of them, "I'll guarantee you, there's somebody else out there who will want to do it."

None of them was selected for the top spot. Robert C. Wright, head of GE's financial operations, was eventually appointed – somebody Welch could trust to carry out his leadership philosophy, and who did so with consummate success. No taken-over executive can claim, however, that

New broom
Robert C. Wright left GE's financial services to become head of NBC television, acquired as part of RCA in 1986, vaulting over the heads of the NBC managerial hierarchy then in place.

Welch as leader is any more demanding with them than with insiders – including himself. The demands include the stipulation that senior executives should strive to develop their own excellent replacements.

Looking to the future

Welch's approach to his own succession bears some similarity to the often criticized four-year process that took him to the top of the company. The method is "to put lots of people in lots of different jobs... and have the board and the senior management team look at them and see how they perform under all kinds of different circumstances." Managers who perform well in some circumstances may not do so in others.

"Some people can do just fine as long as the growth curve's growing," says Welch, "but when all hell breaks loose, you see them change their whole personality. Some can adapt to any situation." Even when you have observed people over time, however, selection is not scientific. In the end, you have to "take a guess and pray you're right."

When Welch succeeded Reg Jones, the latter deliberately sought a leader possessing very different qualities to his own. The excellence of his choice of Welch is an exception to the general rule that CEOs should never choose their own successor; without meaning to, they usually pick somebody whose record will not outshine theirs. Welch's ideas about his own successor, however, sound like a self-portrait. Among the characteristics he seeks are:

- Incredible energy
- Ability to excite others
- Ability to define a vision

■ Finding change fun and not paralyzing
■ Feeling comfortable in Delhi or Denver
■ Ability to talk to all kinds of people

Such leaders are not easily found. Welch's own sensational performance as leader was based on his diagnosis of the grave faults that, if left unhealed, would have laid GE low. It seems unlikely that his successor will find similarly easy targets, equally severe faults, to correct. However, as Welch fully knows, the ultimate test of a leader is not what happens during his or her leadership – but what follows after he or she has departed.

Ideas into action

■ Develop a vision for the business, and change the culture to achieve the vision.

■ Insist that managers share their ideas, information, and experiences with their colleagues.

■ Let people manage their delegated business as they see fit.

■ "Ginger up" management by making unexpected visits and engaging in confrontational argument.

■ Fix goals for all important measures, and treat them as solid commitments that management must keep.

■ Brief yourself fully on everybody who works for you and make sure you recognize them.

■ Be tough, but do not be hard, with everyone with whom you have dealings.

Taking the helm at General Electric

Jack Welch's advent in 1981 was not warmly welcomed. Executives assembled at the training HQ at Croton-on-Hudson, NY, showed little sympathy for his strategy of reducing the workforce and restructuring the portfolio.

Welch recalls the occasion: "I went there when 60 percent of the audience would sneer at me. Most of them wondered, 'Is this guy a nut? Should he be arrested?' It was difficult."

His path through the difficulties, however, was dead straight. Welch took into his management philosophy ideas that he had learned, more or less literally, at his mother's knee. As his tenure as CEO drew toward its end in 2000, these were still his governing principles:

- Face reality as it is, not as you wish it were.
- Be candid with everyone.
- Don't manage, lead.
- Change before you have to.
- If you don't have a competitive advantage, don't compete.
- Control your own destiny, or someone else will.

None of these six principles was compatible with the bureaucracy that Welch had experienced in his rise through GE's ranks. Welch made clear his feelings about his legacy, which the company's fine but aging skyscraper in New York (see right) could be seen to symbolize:

"The cramping artifacts that pile up in the dusty attics of century-old companies: reports, meetings, rituals, approvals, and forests of paper that seem necessary until they are removed."

Welch set out to remove them – even though many had been added by the former CEO, Reginald Jones, who picked Welch as his successor. Under Jones's regime, one GE business alone generated seven daily reports, each of them 12 ft (3.6 m) high.

Forcing the pace

The new man cut a wide swath, not only through the paper, but the whole organization of long-service people: they averaged 13 years of service with a company that they did not want to see change. But their CEO calculated that GE needed to

> **"Incremental change doesn't work very well in the type of transformation GE has gone through. If your change isn't big enough, revolutionary enough, the bureaucracy can beat you."** *Jack Welch Speaks*

increase profits by 4.5 to 6 percent annually – up to double the probable growth of the US economy – to meet his ambitions for the company. This was far higher than GE's own planners thought feasible, and in 1982 revenues in fact fell slightly. All this only confirmed Welch's view that radical restructuring was essential to cut costs, obtain regular quarterly rises in earnings, create a dynamic future for the company, and enrich the investors.

His major weapon was to become a famous one – the rule of "number one or number two." Unless a company either led its market or was a good second, or could rise to that position, and also had the financial results that should accompany such strength, Welch would close or sell the business. Wielding this bludgeon, whatever the internal opposition, achieved the rapid transformation that the CEO wanted – and placed him firmly and permanently in command.

Exercising leadership

Leaders set the direction for the people and the organizations they lead, integrating new-style management skills with traditional demands. Assess and build on your leadership qualities, and master the art of running a team and optimizing individual performance to get collective success.

Managing and leading

The pressures on managers are changing dramatically. Managers today are expected to have mastered all the traditional techniques of management – of implementation, maintenance, and watching the bottom line – but also to have mastered the new-style management skills that make them leaders, people who think for themselves.

Management Techniques	
Old-style management skills	**New-style management skills**
Planning	Counseling groups
Organizing	Providing resources
Implementing	Encouraging ideas
Measuring	Thinking for yourself

Using all the skills

Mastery of all the old-style management skills was crucial to Jack Welch in bringing dramatic change to GE. Welch:

■ Planned: "Be number 1 or 2 in your global market or else" is strategic planning at its best – short, sharp, and to the point.

■ Organized: Welch restructured GE into a dozen businesses with no supervisory layer between him and the business leaders.

■ Implemented: Welch put his "big, big ideas," such as Work-Out and Six Sigma, into operation within months.

■ Measured: Welch put measures on everything by which he wanted to judge performance.

However, the new-style techniques he now restlessly encourages in his managers are indispensable in a fast-moving business world and are far better suited to developing the full strengths of an organization.

Personal attributes

New-style ideals, like old-style managing, are only as valuable as the energy with which you pursue them. Welch is a superlative example of how greatly leadership revolves around personal attributes. Excellent ideas, of course, are indispensable, but you will not translate them into excellent action without the qualities that Welch admires in leaders. Test your own attributes. Do you have:

- Enormous energy and passion for the job?
- An ability to excite, energize, and mobilize an organization?
- The understanding that the customer is the arbiter of performance and the source of profit?
- Technical grasp backed by strong financial understanding?
- A desire to achieve better profits through better products, services, and processes?

Developing your leadership skills

If you do not possess all of the above attributes, do not despair. Some people are natural-born leaders, but you can develop any of the five attributes if you have the desire to lead and are willing to work at it.

Develop Your Leadership Abilities

Write down what you really like about your job. Think up a project that uses these features and try to bring it to life.

Put together a "hot group" to execute the project. Set demanding deadlines, with the group's agreement, and delegate tasks to members, with clear responsibilities.

Make sure that the project will generate real benefits for customers (internally or externally) and will pay off handsomely.

Ensure that you know as much as anybody, if not more, about the technical and financial aspects of the project.

Plan for its further development to generate still better results.

It is true that you risk failure when you take an initiative like this. But you cannot become an effective leader unless you are prepared sometimes to fail on the way to overall success.

1 Leading a team

Every leader has both a task to complete and a team to lead. To live up to the expectations of a Jack Welch, you must not only produce your personal best: you must also work as the team member who gets top results from the whole team.

Practicing leadership

As team leader, your two prime, linked jobs are to decide what needs to happen and to make it happen. Both jobs operate through six highly practical channels: meetings, communications, delegation, approvals, ideas, and relationships. When operating in any of these channels of leadership, always proceed by using six key steps.

The Six Key Steps
Pick the right people.
Have a clear purpose.
Put it in writing.
Work to a strict timetable.
Plan action.
Act on the plan.

Leading meetings

The first channel — meetings — are often led ineffectually. Make sure with every meeting that you follow the six key steps. Ensure that:

- all those present have a reason for being there and a role to play — which they actually do play.
- there is a clear purpose and a written agenda, distributed beforehand with full supporting papers.
- meetings start and finish on time.
- you end up with an action plan, with deadlines and designated responsibilities.
- you set up feedback to ensure that actions are taken — or modified if necessary.

Achieving positive results

Taking the right steps will not of itself make you a successful team leader. The world is full of leaders who run meetings well, communicate effectively, give or withhold approvals rapidly, have plenty of good ideas, and get along well with everybody – but who have failed or are failing. You must get good outcomes.

To get positive results from your team you must behave positively. If your behavior is negative you will achieve only mediocre results. How positive is your behavior? Study the two columns below and score yourself separately on each count. For each negative or positive conduct, score 0 for Never, 1 for Sometimes, and 2 for Always.

Negative behavior	Positive behavior
■ Ignoring values	■ Living the values
■ Being a bureaucrat	■ Being an entrepreneur
■ Underachieving	■ Hitting high targets
■ Starting slowly	■ Starting decisively
■ Changing reluctantly	■ Embracing change
■ Words, not action	■ Doing what you say
■ Lacking focus	■ Concentrating focus
■ Not acting on the facts	■ Managing on the facts
■ Blaming others	■ Forgiving honest error
■ Mismanaging time	■ Organizing yourself

Total each column, then subtract your Negative behavior total from your Positive total. If your score is below 20, start making improvements to advance toward the highest standards of leadership.

The Impact of Positive Behaviour

When Carl Schlemmer made a huge error of judgment, Welch supported him and Schlemmer went on to turn failure into success.

Schlemmer led the team running GE's locomotive business. In 1979, with Welch's approval, they embarked on a $300 million investment built around the "Dash 8" model, predicting a doubled market. In fact, by 1986, the market had fallen by three-quarters.

Welch forgave this honest error and, instead of giving up, Schlemmer focused the team's energies on drastic restructuring. They cut expenses even faster than the fall in sales. By 1987, profits were almost as high as they were before the fall.

2 Picking winners

Leaders are ultimately only as good as the people who follow their lead – and who succeed them. Concentrate a great deal of your time and attention on selecting and developing leaders and potential leaders. You and your organization cannot afford to do otherwise.

Objective assessments

To select potential leaders from your team, make an objective assessment of each candidate's current performance according to specific "hard" and "soft" criteria.

It is not always easy to be objective about people's performance, even on hard, objective measures, such as financial results or market share. Soft, subjective criteria are at least as important but even more difficult to judge. Is it possible to put a number on how open somebody is or how directly people face reality? Welch told his staff: "You're going to have to. Come up with the best numbers you can, and then we'll argue about them."

Rating potential leaders

Go through the same exercise, because objective company results flow from the subjective behaviors of employees. Write down the qualities you want from an appointee to a leadership position, then rate each candidate according to the qualities that they have displayed in their current job.

Your criteria might be covered by the following eight questions. Award points for each on a scale of 0 for "not at all" to 5 for "wholly."

1 Are they power-oriented?
2 Are they fair?
3 Do they protect their territory?
4 Are they self-confident?
5 Are they mean-spirited?
6 Are they open?
7 Do they believe in keeping up barriers?
8 Do they see reality as it really is?

JACK WELCH

Analysis

Subtract the scores for odd-numbered questions from those for even numbers.

- 15 to 20: an excellent candidate with good leadership abilities.
- 6 to 14: a candidate with potential but probably not yet ready for promotion.
- 0 to 5: a candidate without leadership potential.

Thorough investigation

If you are unable to rate a candidate, investigate further. Welch teaches that you can never devote too much time to getting the right people in the right positions. That is why he holds exhaustive Session C reviews (see p. 23) of all top-echelon managers.

To match Welch's thoroughness, subject the members of your own team to the same painstaking analysis of their accomplishments.

Accomplishment Analysis

Produce a full, fair report on people's strengths and weaknesses, including your assessment of their development needs.

Give them the report and discuss its findings.

Get them to appraise themselves – and read and discuss that document, too.

Demanding high standards

As part of your thorough assessment of candidates, you should adhere rigidly to the Can Do, Will Do guide. Welch makes no exceptions on this matter and neither should you.

Evaluation guide

This simple matrix will resolve most of your people decisions. How do employees rate on ability and motivation? Let that rating guide your actions.

- Value employees who Can Do and Will Do, and reward them with training, promotion, and stock options.
- Train those who Will Do but Can't Do.
- Motivate or fire all those who Can Do but Won't Do.
- Let go those who Can't Do and Won't Do.

2

Mobilizing the workforce

Hitting the home run for your company ● Creating competitive strength by making the company leaner and fitter — and keeping it that way ● **How to target the limitless potential for higher productivity** ● Taking out the boss element and removing the "whips and chains" ● **How to make it compulsory to share people-based values** ● The Work-Out method for improving performance and mobilizing participation ● **Learning and applying lessons from other companies** ● How quality can be a unifying force

If gratifying the shareholders is the only test of a chief executive, Jack Welch's management ideas, and their execution, must be pronounced a triumph. To delight shareholders, however, a CEO need only preside over exceptional rises in the share price. Welch made this increase in shareholder wealth, or the value of the company, his great ultimate objective. He would be quick to say, however, that other interests have to be satisfied in other ways first – especially those of the workforce.

How to mobilize and satisfy employees (200,000 to 300,000 over the course of his tenure) is an area in which Welch has made some of his most cogent contributions to management thought and practice. Yet in his early years, Welch's reputation for good management was at best uncertain, largely because of his treatment of labor.

Cutting out corporate fat

As "Neutron Jack" Welch sold, closed, and "restructured" businesses (or cut back their employment), the job cuts were not the only cause for bitter complaint. The unions were pressured to agree to wage and benefit cuts and reformed working practices. Such actions are guaranteed to produce unrest, but as Welch told *Business Week*, he refused to accept that morale was suffering as a result: "I don't sense that. I sense a rapidly escalating appreciation for the world competitive market, and for what we have to do to work smarter together."

The quotation, if optimistic at the time, sums up Welch's philosophy. His attitude to fellow employees is the same from top executive right through to the shop floor. The corporate staff, in fact, were cut by two-fifths to 1,000 immediately as Welch took over – proportionately a far larger cut than the 100,000 cuts (25 percent) on the shop floor between 1981 and 1987. To Welch, competitive strength is all. Excessive numbers make costs uncompetitive, and bad working practices hamstring productivity. Whatever the passing pain, he believes that people who find themselves working more effectively in a leaner and fitter business will eventually respond positively. Welch expressed himself thus: "You want to open up the place so people can flower and grow, expand, hit the home run. When you're tight-bound, controlled, checked, nitpicked, you kill it."

Improving employee value

For all that, many years after the Neutron Jack days the same criticisms more than lingered on. In mid-1998, an important union organizer told *Business Week* that: "No matter how many records are broken in productivity or profits, it's always 'What have you done for me lately?' The workers are considered lemons, and they are squeezed really dry." To that, Welch would reply in two halves. He would reject the squeezed lemon analogy; and he would argue strenuously that it truly doesn't matter how many records are broken in productivity or profits – it is always possible, indeed essential, to do better still.

On this argument, the alternative to Welch's vision of a highly competitive, aggressive, driven hyperperformer is not a benevolent, collaborative, harmonious, all-around center of excellence: the alternative is failure. The workforce plays a crucial part in following the only winning way. That is not only because labor costs loom large in the corporate budget (they averaged 40 percent of costs in GE when Welch took over, although in some businesses labor represents a tiny percentage of total spending). Even more important, the way in which employees work has a profound impact on performance – and on its potential for unbounded improvement:

"The facts are, it's limitless. Our productivity is at the beginning stages. There's so much waste. There's so much more to get, it's unbelievable. And somehow or other, people think all these things are finite."

That quotation does not refer to Welch's early, pre-reform days, but to much later. There are two approaches to workforce productivity. The first, or Neutron Jack, phase is about cutting, making a company leaner and fitter by obvious, sweeping actions that involve major losses of jobs. Once management has "taken out the fat" (Welch's words), that route has reached a dead end. At that point, management must change gear to travel a new road.

Banishing traditional bosses

Following that route places heavy demands on management as well as labor. In 1991 Welch declared that "We've got to take out the boss element. We're going to win on our ideas, not by whips and chains" – one of his most pregnant remarks. Without that massive cultural shift, he did not believe that GE could arrive at his three ideals of "speed, simplicity, and self-confidence." While not

"**For a lean organization, the only route to productivity is to build an energized, involved, participative, turned-on workforce, where everyone plays a role, where every idea counts.**" *Control Your Destiny or Someone Else Will* (1993)

sacrificing any of his emphasis on profit to those three virtues, Welch clearly saw that concentrating mainly on the delivery of short-term results – even excellent ones – was inimical to his new ideas. Only changed managers could lead a changed workforce.

Managers and other employees, he argues, must act boldly outside functional boxes and traditional lines of authority in a climate of learning and sharing. Otherwise, the long-term interests of a company will suffer, and the people-based management that Welch considers vital for productivity cannot become a reality. This is not an issue of motivating and empowering alone. Management determines productivity, not only by these "soft" processes, but also by the "hard" production and other systems that it establishes and supervises.

Studying GE practices

In 1988–89, an internal GE "Best Practices" study showed, for example, that GE's new product development had been counterproductive. The developers had looked for great leaps forward, but the study report pointed to a superior strategy – that is, to plan ahead in stages, with each version of the product making controlled advances on its predecessor. That way, products get to market faster, and sudden technological crashes are avoided. It turned out, too, that GE's celebrated habit of rotating executives fast from job to job was also counter-productive. Among other things, it slowed new product development. Both defects had a serious impact on the performance figures attributed to employees; unless the system under which they work is changed, however, they are powerless to improve their contribution.

Handling executives

Effective people management does not end with installing the most effective and economic system, or with meeting targets. Delivering on commitments – financial or otherwise – is not enough. Managers, however good at delivery, must show that they share the company's people-based values.

High-achievers at GE who act counter to the values can expect short shrift. They typically breach the behavior on which Welch insists: they force performance out of people rather than inspire it. Welch describes them with the words "autocrat, big shot, tyrant," and finds the titles intolerable. In his 1995 annual report, he duly pronounced sentence on all managers who would not or could not accept GE's people-based values. As one former GE executive commented: "The Welch theory is that those who do, get; those who don't, go."

JACK WELCH

Cultural revolution

The company did not want bosses who won results "without regard to values, and in fact often diminish them by grinding people down, squeezing them, stifling them." Some of the tyrants learned to change. Those who

"Every organization needs values, but a lean organization needs them even more. When you strip away the support systems of staffs and layers, people have to change their habits and expectations, or else the stress will just overwhelm them." *Jack Welch Speaks*

did not were dismissed: "it had to be done if we wanted GE people to be open, to speak up, to share." Welch was mounting a cultural revolution, and resistance was not acceptable. In 1991, Welch explained to *Fortune* that:

"The only ideas that count are the A ideas. There is no second place. That means we have to get everybody in the organization involved. If you do that right, the best ideas will rise to the top."

With that greater involvement in mind, he launched new initiatives to accomplish three purposes:

- Involve employees in decision-making.
- Transfer ideas quickly between different businesses and different departments.
- Simplify production and other processes.

Working with Work-Outs

Company efficiency was to benefit from three initiatives: Work-Outs, Best Practices, and Process Mapping, in which a process is followed diagrammatically from start to finish, and then replanned and redrawn to simplify and speed up the operation. The last two contribute powerfully to the first. Work-Outs, started in March 1989, were designed for a purpose that goes beyond their immediate achievements. They produce short-term improvements in efficiency and costs, while serving a long-term educational aim. Their methodology is easily imitated, dear to Welch's heart and mind, and basic to the cultural revolution he is imposing on GE.

Basically, the unit boss takes some 40–100 staff from all levels to spend three days in informal session off-site, at a conference center or hotel. The boss sets the agenda, which might deal broadly with cutting down on meetings and paperwork, or with more technical matters to do with product and production. After a "town meeting" in which everybody considers the agenda, the group splits into teams, which for two days work on their part of the agenda with a facilitator – and with the boss conspicuously absent.

On the third day the boss returns to hear the proposals – which can number over a hundred. The great majority of these team proposals will be accepted, and very quickly. A key principle in Work-Out, important psychologically as well as practically, is that the manager, listening to his subordinates' proposals at the front of the room, can only say "Yes" or "No" – or request a specified delay, of a month or less, for gathering more information. This insistence reflects Welch's own attitude to decision-making. As one management consultant told *Business Week* in 1998: "Welch will say 'Yes.' Welch will say 'No.' But he never says 'Maybe.'"

From trivial to fundamental

The CEO, of course, will be deciding on greater matters than, for example, new protective shields for grinding machines. That was the biggest saver ($80,000) in the 1991 proposals from one unit's Work-Outs, which cut costs in total by $200,000.

The individual sums saved by Work-Out sessions are not huge, although they get multiplied by many Work-Outs all over GE. The main benefit to the company is psychological and cultural. Welch uses Work-Outs to recreate the same no-holds-barred atmosphere that he famously enjoys so wholeheartedly in his confrontations with GE executives in "The Pit," a large amphitheater at the Croton-on-Hudson Management Development Institute, or Crotonville.

Work-Outs start as highly artificial activities, unfamiliar and unsettling to both boss and bossed. Until trust has been built, the impact of the process is limited. But dealing with what Welch calls "administrivia" (like unwanted forms) is more important than it seems. It produces quick victories and prepares people for the tougher stuff: "If you jump right into complicated issues," says Welch, "no one speaks up, because these ideas are more dangerous." The Work-Out process crosses functional boundaries in what can be a threatening manner, and inevitably involves implied and explicit criticism of current management.

Extending Work-Out benefits

In a more advanced phase, teams are drawn, not from different parts of the unit, but from co-workers or people employed along the same "value chain" of linked, sequential processes. Customers and suppliers can be added to the team for mutual benefit. Nor do the teams rest content with generating ideas internally. The business development staff, whose major activity is studying other companies as acquisition targets, has also sought to identify those companies' "best practices" – approaches that could be emulated by GE on an exchange basis.

"[We] like to say 'Work-Out blew up the building.' Consider a building: It has walls and floors; the walls divide the functions, the floors separate the levels. Work-Out took out the floors and walls, leaving all the bodies in one big room."
Jack Welch Speaks

Exchanging practices

Best practice exchanges can take place both externally and internally. For example, a GE appliance plant in Canada successfully adopted the operating ideas of a small New Zealand manufacturer. What happened next graphically illustrates the changes Welch wants and the processes that satisfy his wishes. A senior vice-president visiting the Canadian site saw that the new working methods offered huge potential for GE's giant (and then troubled) Appliance Park in Louisville, Kentucky. He set in motion a program that covered ways to:

- Cut the time from order to production by 90 percent.
- Get the key and most costly 5 percent of components delivered as needed – "just in time."
- Design models to share components.
- Stock parts on the line, not in stores.
- Speed up "changeovers," when the line switches from one model to another.

The changes at Louisville were accomplished through Work-Out "town meetings," plus study trips to Canada for managers and employees (including union shop stewards). The gains at Louisville returned the $3 million cost of the so-called "Quick Response" program a hundred-fold. But to Welch, the results mean far more than that. The progress at Appliance Park, as at many other GE sites, is yet another step toward developing "people whose real income is secure because they're winning, and whose psychic income is rising because every person is participating."

Although Work-Out has such importance in Welch's plans for mobilizing and motivating everybody in the company, its ambitions were transcended by the Six Sigma quality crusade that he launched in 1998 (see p. 50). By commanding every GE business to pursue the Six Sigma goal of no more than 3.4 defects per million parts or operations, Welch aimed to kill several birds with one stone. Major cost savings would flow from huge gains in productivity (for defective output has to be remedied or replaced); and the resulting profit increases would be enhanced by higher customer satisfaction.

Moreover, the detailed training for Six Sigma projects, followed by their execution, would indoctrinate and enthuse employees as they learned how much they could do, as individuals and in teams, to transform performance. When Welch picks 29 managers to sing their Six Sigma successes before 471 peers gathered at Boca Raton, he is not only encouraging the propagation and sharing of quality ideas. He is sustaining the top-down pressure for greater efficiencies and wider effectiveness – and encouraging others to spread the message in turn.

Unifying to achieve quality

As Janet C. Lowe reported in her 1998 book, *Jack Welch Speaks*, Welch told her: "It's the job of the leader, the job of the manager, the job of the employee – everyone's job is quality." This would hardly have come as news to Welch's Japanese peers, or to any of the millions of Americans who in 1970 watched a TV documentary that shook corporate America with its revelations about Japan's vast superiority in quality. It remains a mystery why Welch, with his enthusiasm for borrowing "best practice" ideas from elsewhere, took so long to imitate Japanese quality methods, which had actually been inspired in the early post-war years by an American, W. Edwards Deming.

Japanese wake-up call
Welch's drive to involve everyone at GE in the Six Sigma quality-improvement program was spurred by the knowledge that Japan had far outstripped the US in delivering top quality.

Welch, however, expropriated Six Sigma almost as a proprietary product for GE. As he explained in Robert Slater's book, *Jack Welch and the GE Way*, it started as a quality program; then "we turned it into an internal productivity program, saving waste and all that, then we turned it to our customers." Thus, in 2000 GE started measuring Six Sigma success by monitoring customer satisfaction, and not just monetary savings. But Six Sigma transcends even the cause of customer satisfaction: "It's the most important management training thing we've ever had. It's better than going to Harvard Business School. It's better than Crotonville. It teaches you how to think differently." He believes that this is "changing the fundamental DNA of the company."

Welch puts forward the achievements of GE as undeniable evidence that making changes in attitudes and environment is both possible and highly effective. He believes that Neutron Jack has been left far behind, that he has "proved that productivity is not a matter of cut and burn." Motivating the workforce to achieve "has nothing to do with whips and chains. It's a never-ending process that's based on empowerment. It's what happens when you get people excited about finding solutions to their problems."

Ideas into action

- Go for the three-S ideals of speed, simplicity, and self-confidence.

- Outlaw autocracy and tyranny to help people to be open, to speak up, and to share.

- Insist that managers (including yourself) make their decisions clearly and quickly.

- Start off improvement teams on quick fixes, including elimination of "administrivia."

- Adopt total quality methods to save costs, raise productivity, and delight customers.

- Never relent in the insistent pursuit of better personal and company performance.

- Use quality programs as the key means of management development.

Finding the Six Sigma quality principle

Jack Welch was actually absent on the day that Six Sigma came to GE and changed it forever. When the 30-strong Corporate Executive Council was meeting in June 1995, he was recovering from a heart operation.

The hit speaker at Crotonville was a close friend, Lawrence A. Bossidy, a former vice-chairman of GE. Bossidy, now CEO of Allied-Signal, sang the praises of the radical quality program he had introduced there: Six Sigma. As he explained, any activity that generates fewer than 3.4 defects per million manufactured parts (or the equivalent in services) merits the technical description, Six Sigma.

In August, when the returned Welch heard about Bossidy's reception, he responded with enthusiasm. In fact, GE was surprisingly (and very) late in joining the quality movement. Motorola, as the leading example, had already been pursuing Six Sigma for a whole decade. But Welch showed his typical drive. Before the year ended, GE had 200 projects under way.

The projects were to be backed by intensive training. Employees have to master statistical and other techniques, and the effort must be led by highly trained people: using judo terms, GE called the latter "master black belts, black belts, and green belts." In 1996, the first full year, the project total soared to 3,000, and in 1997 it doubled. The payoff was estimated at $320 million in higher productivity and profits. While this figure was double Welch's original target, it was still far short of the total deficit between Six Sigma and actual performance: a gap somewhere between $8 billion and $12 billion annually.

Six Sigma successes

The achievements that GE can attribute to the Six Sigma program so far include:

- A 98 percent cut in defects on a billing system used in transactions with the Wal-Mart store chain (see right).
- A cut in preparation time for one jet engine from two days to some 10 hours.
- A cut in chest-scan time from three minutes to 17 seconds.

Welch, however, wanted intangibles as much as the tangibles. He seized on Six Sigma as a way of uniting management and workforce in the practical, continuous pursuit of lower costs and higher efficiencies – the ideal killer combination that he had been advocating since taking over. His vehemence on the issue can be ferocious. After one diatribe in 1999, Welch explained that "the only way I can get attention around here is not to be rational."

Still, the sight of senior managers vying with each other to boast about their Six Sigma

"We want to make our quality so special, so valuable to our customers, so important to their success, that our products become their only real value choice."
Jack Welch Speaks

gains was balm to Welch's heart and more than justified his efforts in support of the program. "Six Sigma has spread like wildfire across the company," he announced in *Fortune* magazine, "and it is transforming everything we do."

3

Winning competitive advantage

How the team with diverse, combined strengths always takes the trophy ● Being number one or number two in the market — and exiting if you are not ● **The necessities of battling with giants** ● Why worker empowerment and liberation are competitive essentials ● **Why cutting costs, and then cutting them again, is crucially important** ● Setting out to triple the annual rate of increase in productivity ● **Running a multibillion conglomerate with a "grocery store" mentality**

J ack Welch is a fierce believer in competition, but only in competition that he can win. He sees no advantage in fighting what are doomed to be losing battles. His directive, "be number one or number two in your market, or else," expressed a strongly held philosophy that sprang from his earlier experiences at General Electric. Unlike many executives in the company, he had run high-growth businesses like plastics, and seen "opportunities in wonderful things like GE Capital." Rapid growth and great opportunities excited him personally – and they were plainly the way to create corporate success.

On the other hand, as a corporate vice-president, Welch also had big, bureaucratic businesses a century old reporting to him: "I saw businesses that ... we were holding on to as a shrine to our past." GE had trained Welch in good businesses, as well as bad, while other managers never saw a good one, and Welch felt sorry for them.

Simplifying the strategy

T hese bad businesses were only compared with their direct competitors. If their returns were 9 percent on capital and their competitor in the same industry earned 7 percent, they thought they were doing well. "The fact that they should be getting 15 percent was difficult to comprehend." Welch could not abide this satisfaction with inadequate returns. Hence his fourfold thrust to:

- Ensure that GE only operated in the right, good sectors.
- Move into growth businesses with competitive advantage.
- Organize the company to respond rapidly to change.
- Use the three far-reaching reforms above to earn greater returns on capital.

The sky was the limit for those returns. Welch wanted to make "as much out of the capital employed as we could." This simplistic financial strategy was not based on the kind of intellectual analysis for which GE's army of corporate planners (nearly all now axed) had been famed. Complex concepts like Economic Value Added and Market Value Added have since formalized the need for companies to earn more than their cost of capital. But "We didn't understand EVA and MVA or any of these things," says Welch.

Playing to win

What he did understand to the core of his being was that companies got into trouble by investing a lot of capital, and getting little from it. At GE, using capital efficiently became a driving force. Losses are not efficient uses of capital. However, Welch's competitive drive has sometimes taken him into areas where loss is possible. Here he would rather play than give up: "I like to fight like hell before I lose." He would always prefer to pick something else, though. The exceptions prove the important rule cited earlier: "Don't play with businesses that can't win."

Winning the competitive fights does not mean picking on somebody smaller than yourself. Few companies in the world are bigger than GE. Its opposition, however, can muster great strengths: "We compete with giants. So we have an enemy, if you will. We compete with companies and governments." He is far from being afraid of government-backed competition, however. Welch believes that the free enterprise system in America is freer than any other and a potential source of great competitive advantage.

There is a threat to this strength: "If we put bureaucracy and rigidity into our system, we play into our competitors' hands in global markets." He sees US companies as lacking the benefits of protected markets, government support, and political favors. This is a view that non-US competitors would certainly not share, to put it mildly. But it reinforces Welch's argument for his own policies: "if we let our people flourish and grow, if we use the best ideas they come up with, then we have the chance to win."

Winning worldwide

His drive to liberate and empower the workforce (see p. 38) is therefore not enlightened management for enlightenment's sake: "it's a competitive necessity. When you look at the global arena, that's what our competitive advantage is. We have got to unleash it." Welch had seized on the fact that in the global economy, no corporation can be an island unto itself.

Accordingly, early on in his reign, he modified the famous "number one or number two" rule. Originally, GE businesses had to seek this ranking in their domestic markets. Welch changed the stipulation to the whole world market. This was not just a matter of semantics. Welch's globalism dates back to 1985, when revenues outside the US were only a fifth of the corporate total. The proportion was

"There will only be one standard for corporate success: international market share.... The winning corporations – those which can dictate their destiny – will win by finding markets all over the world." *Control Your Destiny or Someone Else Will*

little higher two years later. By 1998, however, global sales came to $42.8 billion, more than total revenues in 1987, and representing over two-fifths of the total.

To put that another way, GE's sales rose by $60.1 billion between 1987 and 1998. Over half that increase came from abroad, with Europe supplying the lion's share of the sales. The principles were strong, direct, and simple:

- Move into global markets fast and powerfully.
- Build a solid, domestic base before launching the attack.
- Use acquisitions to create or enlarge a bridgehead.
- Strengthen underperforming businesses by acquisition and pooling assets.
- Concentrate on major businesses where you can win (in GE's case, that meant seven global activities ranging from jet engines to medical systems).
- Develop local management, and bring expatriates home as soon as possible.

The key to the global takeoff was a 1987 swap deal for which Welch was widely criticized. The French company Thomson ceded ownership of its medical imaging business, which greatly strengthened GE's position in the European market. In return, Thomson took over TV manufacture from GE. This provoked protests from many about surrender of key US businesses to foreign competition. But Welch knew exactly what he was doing when he made the deal. A primarily domestic, low-growth business suffering from intense competition is not his idea of a strong strategic asset. A global business specializing in a high-growth, high-profit field meets his prescription exactly.

Welch regards globalization as a three-stage process. First, "we started out going after markets and expanding our horizons.... Then we took globalization to the next step, which was globalizing components, products... sourcing around the world." The third step is "globalizing the intellect." Speaking in Robert Slater's *Jack Welch and the GE Way*, he mentioned Indian research laboratories, Russian scientists and materials, and various "medical centers of excellence" — the emphasis is "local, local."

Cutting the costs

Welch puts his businesses through a tough catechism that gives a clear picture of his nakedly competitive thrust. The questions asked are not comfortable. Nor are they asked — though they should be — by all CEOs:

- What does your global competitive environment look like?
- In the last three years, what have your competitors done to you?
- In the same period, what have you done to them?
- How might they attack you in the future?
- What are your plans to leapfrog them?

As the catechism shows, Welch's strategy is founded on a refusal to let his company join the usual procession of competitors, marching abreast with much the same product offers, winning some contracts and losing others. He wants to differentiate and to win. To that end, Welch preaches (and tries very hard to practice) both high performance and low cost, but with the final emphasis on the latter. If you want to sell turbines to developing countries, for example, you very probably have to operate from a low cost base.

It follows logically that the businesses have to be more productive, not just compared to their own past records, but compared to the best competitors. To Welch, cost is a driver that you have to keep benchmarking – making comparisons with the best you can, and cutting costs to the best levels anywhere, whatever the impact in human terms.

After the purchase in 1985 of RCA (when six major businesses were sold or closed, affecting 41,000 employees), Welch's people found 700 job cuts even at RCA's broadcasting arm – and NBC was supposed to have the lowest costs in the business. Welch does not reshuffle GE's businesses simply to save costs, however: the real purpose is to sharpen their competitive edge.

Welch pointed out in 1995 that a refrigerator cost about the same price as when he was appointed CEO. In contrast, the price of an automobile had risen something like two-and-a-half times since 1981. In many industries marked by severe competition, US companies have conspicuously failed to meet the challenge of increasing margins and returns on capital. Not so at GE. Welch reckons that the price index for GE's product range in 1989–95 was probably negative; yet its profits grew at double-digit rates. "That comes from using capital more efficiently, using people more efficiently, from systems behavior."

Welch's overarching goal went much further, however. It was nothing less than to become "the most competitive enterprise on this earth." In a sense, the goal is more important than its attainment. That is because the goalposts are always being moved, sometimes by the actions of

"In the end, you could have performance, you can have quality, but you'd better have cost." *Control Your Destiny or Someone Else Will*

competitors, sometimes by changes in technology, sometimes by developments in markets. Welch thus committed GE to a relentless pursuit of unachievable perfection. He drove the company to:

- Achieve the industry's lowest costs.
- Increase sales by creating new markets.
- Lead the world in customer service, with sophisticated fulfillment and distribution systems.
- Lead in product quality.
- Raise productivity.

Productivity power

From early on, Welch aimed to triple GE's annual rate of productivity increase – a huge ambition. The link between productivity and competitiveness is obvious to any manager, but to Welch productivity goes deeper still: "When a business becomes productive, it gains control of its destiny." That is the justification for putting a company through the pain of restructuring:

"... you go through trauma, you bottom out – and then you start to see results. Once you get back to being productive, the jobs come back, you succeed in the marketplace, your profit margins rise. You were hurting for awhile, but now you feel great."

The task of management is to create systems, within a sensibly structured business, that enable people to achieve higher productivity and greater competitive advantage. In their book, *Control Your Destiny or Someone Else Will*, Noel M. Tichy and Stratford Sherman cite the case of a plant that makes wire, another that wraps the wire into coils, and a third that assembles the coils into lamps. If these are organized as three separate businesses, each optimizing its own performance, the totality may well not be optimized. Organized as a single unit, however, those three plants can seek the optimum balance of opportunities: for instance, making a costlier wire may help to produce a cheaper lamp.

Lessons of success

Half-way through Welch's period in office, however, it became apparent that GE's productive systems were defective in key respects. The best practices that GE discovered in other companies in 1988–89 were less technical than managerial. What made some companies successful where others failed? The answers were quite disturbing for GE, which found that it compared badly on eight basic points. It noted that successful companies:

- Managed processes, not people.
- Used techniques (like "process mapping" and "benchmarking") to achieve continuous improvement.
- Valued incremental gains.
- Measured performance by customer satisfaction.
- Introduced new products faster than the competition.
- Designed new products for efficient manufacture.
- Treated suppliers as partners.
- Managed inventory in superior fashion.

The first of these secrets of success was crucial. Learning its lessons, GE shifted from *what* it was doing to *how* it was being done: in other words, it focused on how people produced, not how much. Instead of keeping score and relating results to targets, with a wholly financial staff checking the numbers, the audit staff was changed until half the auditors were operational experts who knew ways to improve the how. But Welch does not rely on staffwork to regulate and raise competitive prowess. That is a job for committed line managers – for leaders.

The CEO himself must be as deeply committed as anybody else, if not more so. Welch believes in trying to know every employee and every customer, just like a village grocer. Welch even nicknames GE "the grocery store":

"What's important at the grocery store is just as important in engines or medical systems. If the customer isn't satisfied, if the stuff is getting stale, if the shelf isn't right, or if the offerings aren't right, it's the same thing. You manage it like a small organization. You don't get hung up on zeros."

The informal approach

Nor do you allow formalities to get in the way. "Jack" to everybody, Welch acts in informal ways and inevitably sets an informal style for others. Welch regards his emphasis on informality as a "big thought." He says: "I don't think people have ever figured out that being informal is a big deal." Informality means a set of key actions by the CEO, all of which heighten competitiveness:

- Breaking the chain of command
- Communicating freely, up and down
- Paying for performance as an entrepreneurial boss would pay
- Achieving wide personal contact
- Making surprise visits
- Ignoring hierarchical layers
- Sending reams of handwritten notes

An excellent example of the CEO's informal but powerful role in pursuing the competition is that of the tubes used for X-rays and CT-scans. In 1993 Welch heard in one of his customer conversations (which take 15–20 percent of his time) that competitive products offered a tube life more than double GE's. Highly displeased, and bypassing two levels in the hierarchy, Welch found the right manager, called him into HQ, and demanded a quadrupling of tube life. According to James A. Byrne, writing in *Business Week* in 1998, the exact words were, "Fix it. I want 100,000 scans out of my tubes!" (note the "my").

Honing the competitive edge

It was much easier said than done. Over four years Welch received weekly reports on progress, to which he replied regularly with handwritten notes alternating praise with impatience. The campaign paid off: tubes finally appeared that lasted for 150,000 and 200,000 scans. The new methods created productivity gains worth some $14 million. You have to wonder at the long gestation, and at the mismanagement that allowed so large a competitive gap to emerge. But you also have to marvel at the persistence with which the CEO pursued improvement at a relatively small operation. That illustrates one of four key aspects of Welch's intensely competitive approach:

- Persistence: you never give up the thrust to achieve a better product, superior marketing, greater internal efficiency, better customer relations, and so on.
- Detail: the leader creates the broad competitive strategy, but uses detailed intervention when necessary to help maintain its integrity.

■ Customer responsiveness: the arbiter of the company's competitive success is the external purchaser, not the internal management.

■ Culture: the persistent, detailed, customer-facing approach of the leader establishes a role model for the whole organization.

That competitive culture is Welch's ultimate weapon in the global wars. His whole time at the top can be seen as a massive effort to prove that big corporations – even one with a quarter of a million employees – can be as pugnacious and responsive as small ones: "We are trying to get the soul and energy of a start-up into the body of a $60 billion, 114-year-old company." Welch's own career had taken off with his transformation of GE's tiny plastics business. He wanted to turn GE into plastics writ large – very large. Not only were major initiatives like Work-Out and Six Sigma, and course after course at Crotonville, enlisted in the cause: Welch doggedly pursued "vision and values" at every opportunity.

Soft values, hard results

These "soft" issues, embedded in carefully crafted "shared statements," are not easily associated with the "hard" management for which Welch has come to be famous. But the values promote what he wants: a company that is lean and agile, that pursues high excellence and high quality, where entrepreneurship is encouraged and practiced, where reality and candor dominate exchanges of all kinds. In this vision, managers are stewards of the owners' assets. They have to deal with paradox as a way of life, to accept that change is continual and nothing is sacred.

There are to be no secrets, but "constructive conflict" has to flourish in the pursuit of customer satisfaction.

In his final decade, Welch began preaching other values, too: respect for others, openness, and "ownership" of jobs, in an atmosphere where every contribution counts. Here Welch is reflecting a critical change of strategic direction. The hard facts of competition remain crucial: but living the softer values that unite the components of a diversified business creates the indispensable difference between big winners and large losers. Welch wants to build a company that, like its leader, competes hard, hates to lose, and is only interested in winning big.

Ideas into action

- Make the return on capital employed as high as you can.

- Do not play with businesses that cannot win the competitive wars.

- Differentiate your business from competitors to make it easier to beat them.

- Commit management to the relentless pursuit of unattainable perfection.

- Seek to optimize the totality of the business rather than the profits of its components.

- Focus on how people are producing, not on how much they produce.

- Establish and share values and practical ideas that will boost competitiveness.

Changing company culture

Transforming an organization may be vital to improving performance. This cannot be accomplished without changing its culture – the values and attitudes shared by its members. To do this, you establish key company values, change the behavior of individuals, and abolish bureaucracy in favor of a creative, enterprising climate of "best practice."

Establishing a new culture

To Jack Welch, reality, candor, and integrity are not ideals but essential weapons in the battle for competitive success and profitable growth. They are fundamental to the culture he established at GE. Do you face reality, tell the truth to everybody (including yourself), and display honesty in all your dealings? If this is not the case, you will not cope well with business needs or earn the trust on which performance ultimately depends.

The role of a values statement

Welch spent years and involved 5,000 people in producing a values statement for GE that made it clear what attitudes and behavior he expected from employees. As more and more of his staff tried to live by these values, they changed the culture of GE. Today every GE manager has a card that reminds them of the values. It states that GE leaders ("always with unyielding integrity"):

- ■ have a passion for excellence and hate bureaucracy.
- ■ are open to ideas from anywhere.
- ■ live quality… and drive cost and speed for competitive advantage.
- ■ have the self-confidence to involve everyone and behave in a boundaryless fashion.
- ■ create a clear, simple, reality-based vision… and communicate it to all constituencies.
- ■ have enormous energy and the ability to energize others.
- ■ stretch… set aggressive goals… reward progress… yet understand accountability and commitment.
- ■ see change as opportunity… not threat.
- ■ have global brains… and build diverse and global teams.

1 Establishing values

Adapt GE's values for your own purposes. Ensure that they are lived by your team or department by producing a workable values statement, and enforce those values by using the three Rs technique (below).

Drawing up a values statement

Before you expect people to live by a values statement, you must make sure it meets six key criteria.

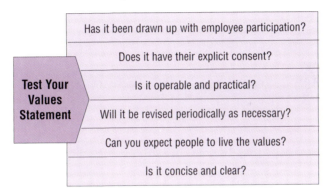

Test Your Values Statement

Has it been drawn up with employee participation?

Does it have their explicit consent?

Is it operable and practical?

Will it be revised periodically as necessary?

Can you expect people to live the values?

Is it concise and clear?

Enforcing values

Maintain commitment to the company values statement by using the Three Rs – Reward, Repetition, and Removal. At GE, Welch fits managers into one of four categories or types. Type I delivers on performance commitments and shares the company's people-based values; Type II does not meet commitments and does not share the values; Type III misses commitments, but shares the values; Type IV delivers on commitments but does not share the values. Each Type requires different treatment. Follow these principles:

- Type I: keep by progressing and promoting (Reward).
- Type II: do not keep in the organization (Removal).
- Type III: give a second chance, preferably in a different environment (Repetition).
- Type IV: provide an opportunity to change their ways (usually very difficult for them) or fire (Repetition or Removal).

Above all, remember the importance of personal example from the leader at all times. This is the fourth R: Role Model.

2 Changing behavior

Fundamental to changing the culture of an organization is altering people's behavior. Welch achieved great success with the introduction of Work-Outs and Six Sigma – and so could you.

Practicing Work-Outs

The Work-Out program (see p. 43) that Jack Welch launched in 1988 was designed to make the behavior of both bosses and bossed more positive, while bringing substantial benefits to the bottom line.

The Purposes of Work-Outs
To develop a climate of trust.
To empower people to improve their own performance.
To cut out wasted work, time, and cost.
To establish a new corporate culture of collaboration and sharing.

These results can be won in any company. Take members of your unit off-site for up to three days and present them with a list of problem areas for discussion. Ask them to recommend reforms, ranking them according to the criteria of payoff and effort.

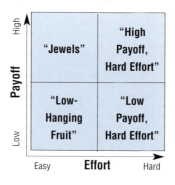

Choosing issues

Place at the top of your list high payoff, easy reforms, known as "jewels." Follow with low payoff, easy reforms, known as "low-hanging fruit."

When delegates make their proposals, reply at once with one of three responses: "Yes," "No," or "Come back with more information inside a month." Implement the accepted proposals.

Achieving Six Sigma

The Six Sigma program (see p. 50) that Jack Welch launched in 1995 comes from the perfectionist world of Total Quality Management. Six Sigma means that 99.999997 percent of what is produced meets specification and is free from defects. Welch regards it as highly educational and a huge force for cultural change. The objectives are common (or should be) to all companies.

The Objectives of Six Sigma
To satisfy the customer.
To reduce the costs.
To improve the quality of purchased supplies.
To lift internal performance.
To enable better performance by better design.

Practicing Six Sigma

To benefit from the Six Sigma approach, you must first insist on measurement of what is being done at present (for example, the percentage of rejects). Next, analyze how performance can be improved, and set new targets that will, when achieved, prove that performance has become markedly better. Then install controls to ensure the operation keeps up the good work. Finally, never give up or let up – there will always be massive improvements possible.

Six Sigma in Action
The application of Six Sigma was crucial to ending the dissatisfaction of GE Lighting's biggest customer – Wal-Mart.

The billing system between GE and the retail giant Wal-Mart was malfunctioning. Faced with disputes, payment delays, and a dissatisfied customer, GE realized that its system required adapting to Wal-Mart's system and needs. Six Sigma was put to work, backed by some IT improvements and $30,000 in investment. Within four months defects came down by 98 percent. Wal-Mart became much happier, and GE Lighting earned back its investment many times over.

2 Beating bureaucracy

All too often minor rules and regulations (and fussy people) that make no sense but seem almost impossible to circumvent can swamp and clog an organization. Learn to identify the classic signs of bureaucracy, and act to eliminate them before the damage is done.

Identifying the disease

How much of your energy is expended on purely internal activities? How much is directed toward exernal customers? If you spend less than 20 percent of your energy on external customers, then bureaucracy has taken hold. Are the classic signs present?

Classic Signs of Bureaucracy
Detailed monthly budget approvals
Centrally-driven strategic planning only
Powerful staff members with no line responsibility
Many-layered approval procedures
Many-layered, strictly observed payment bands
Rigid status symbols
Hefty corporate manuals and "bibles"

Tackling the problems

Bureaucracy makes work and creates a climate in which the customer comes third – well after the management and the company's other employees. Eliminate it as follows:

- Move financial reporting from monthly to quarterly.
- Make senior managers responsible for their own strategies.
- Eliminate all staff jobs unless proved to be essential.
- Push approval levels right down the line.
- Broaden and reduce the payment bands.
- Scrap the status symbols and "burn the bibles."
- Identify nonsenses and eradicate them.

JACK WELCH

3 Becoming the best

Ideas for managing better are one thing you can safely beg, borrow, or steal. If a successful organization anywhere uses practices that you do not, their example may help you reach the same high standards. Adopt their good practices wherever you can.

Using best practice

Many GE businesses employ a tool called the Trotter Matrix to check on their use of best practice. The idea came from Lloyd Trotter, who ran the Electrical Distribution and Controls side of GE. He listed a number of desirable attributes for each of his plants, and then scored each attribute.

The Trotter Scorecard	
0 points	Aware of best practice: no plans to adopt
1 point	Plans to adopt: no current activity
2 points	Current activity on best practice
3 points	Best practice implemented on some product lines
4 points	Best practice implemented on all product lines
5 points	Model site for best practice

Score your own activities on a similar basis. Sadly, most companies earn a zero on everything they do, because they are either unaware of the best practice or else believe they have nothing to learn.

Learning from others

It is only realistic to assume that somebody has found, and is using, better ways for all that you do. Learn from them: most firms are surprisingly generous about letting other managers study their methods. For example, Japanese car makers were perfectly happy to let their Western rivals into their secrets – they knew that by the time the West had followed suit, they would be far ahead, thanks to newer and even better ideas. Avoid the car trap: act fast.

Recreating the role of Crotonville

Before becoming CEO, Jack Welch had never personally attended a course at GE's Management Development Institute in Croton-on-Hudson, NY, the training establishment known as Crotonville.

Welch originally shared his company colleagues' somewhat jaundiced view of Crotonville (see right) as something of a consolation prize for people who had been passed over. But as CEO he realized that he could use the institute as the mainspring of the management system and style he wanted. Crotonville offered a unique and valuable opportunity to indoctrinate the entire GE management corps with his ideas on how a business should be run.

GE's training institute has consequently occupied a major part of his time. In 17 years, the chief executive attended Crotonville 250 times, exposing some 15,000 managers to his ideas – and listening to theirs – in four-hour sessions at which no holds are barred. Welch held that Crotonville would have high academic standards, but its work would not be abstract. The academy would work on GE's strategic issues and would help executives to tackle their own problems directly.

The 70-odd managers who attend the top three-week development program at Crotonville, repeated many times over, are both beneficiaries and missionaries for Welch's ideas – which he delivers in person, usually at the end of the course. Speaking without notes, he expects and welcomes critical, penetrating questions from the students. Spending time socializing with them after business hours, he is there as both boss and professor.

Taking the pulse

The institute also employs the services of numerous academic lecturers, many of them distinguished. It has a large catalog of courses, from entry-level to the above-mentioned, top-level development programs. Welch loves addressing these. He talks with great vigor, but also listens hard because, as he told *Fortune* magazine, the monthly visits are "a great way to take the pulse of the organization."

The revolution sponsored by Welch at Crotonville gave new vigor to GE's reputation as a management pioneer. Welch had scrapped the "Blue Books," five heavy volumes that had been compiled by leading experts, such as Peter Drucker, to guide all GE managers through their work. To Welch, that approach put the cart before the horse. Rather than following the thoughts of others, managers should learn to think for themselves as they tackled their tasks – and should then pass on their thinking. Crotonville made GE the world's supreme example of on-the-job "action learning."

More than symbolically, Crotonville is also the meeting-place for the 30-strong Corporate

"I like it [Crotonville] more and more. I think of it as the most important thing in the transformation. We put money in when we were downsizing the company. We're expanding it." *The GE Way Fieldbook* (2000)

Executive Council, created in 1986 as a quarterly summit forum. The council does not make decisions and has no clear authority to impose its collective will on the GE organization. But this is where Welch and his senior colleagues thrash out the issues, sharing and generating the ideas and policies that will guide GE's future.

4

Pursuing shareholder value

Raising the company's stock market valuation to create wealth ● Making General Electric the world's richest corporation by outgrowing the economy ● **How to restructure a company around core businesses and eliminate noncore ones** ● The concept of the "business engine" as the driver of diversified growth ● **The pursuit of integrated diversity by keeping businesses separate but sharing their strengths** ● Raising the corporate profile by celebrating real achievement

The elevation of "shareholder value" to pole position in the management race became a cliché by the end of the 20th century. The concept did not exist in 1981, when Jack Welch set out to enrich his shareholders beyond their wildest dreams by making General Electric the world's most highly valued company. The market capitalization rose nearly 30 times, adding an astounding, unique $385 billion of shareholder value as Welch dynamically and doggedly pursued the policies that, he believed, would turn his ultimate objective into reality.

Naming the targets

That meant achieving two subordinate targets of equally intimidating size. GE had to outgrow the US and global economies, and its growth rate had to outstrip inflation. Welch wanted no repetition of the previous decade, when growth had narrowly exceeded that of the Gross Domestic Product, but market capitalization had shown no increase at all. He pays informed and incisive attention to the national and world economies and drives GE to adapt dynamically to this environment.

Three elements in his thought thus emerged clearly from the very start of his career as CEO. First, businesses (and managers) must set their own targets. Second, those targets must be "stretch targets," demanding that managers outperform the past and their own expectations. Third, decisions and actions must be directed towards enhancing the real, underlying value of the business in ways that will, in turn, create a richer investment for shareholders (who Welch meaningfully calls "shareowners").

Welch's paradigm of the wealth-creating company has an essentially simple, four-point basis. You should:

Hub of technology
Making jet engines (above) is an activity in which General Electric enjoys definite competitive advantage. Welch led GE away from operations where it could not lead the market.

- Lead the market from a position of number one or number two.
- Achieve "well above average real (that is, after inflation) returns" on investment.
- Have a unique selling proposition based on giving customers value that competitors cannot equal or surpass.
- Build on what the company does best.

In implementing these policies, Welch acts much like an aggressive fund manager who handles a portfolio of shares by deciding which sectors merit investment and buying or selling stocks to meet his financial objectives. In one of Welch's first and most telling analyses, applied a year after taking charge, he divided the company into sharply defined groups. First, he took clearly worthwhile activities and drew three circles round the related businesses. The circles covered, respectively, technology, services, and core manufacturing.

Under technology came medical systems, aircraft engines, and materials. Services included construction and engineering and nuclear services. The core operations were activities such as lighting and transportation (including locomotives). All businesses inside the circles were long-term holdings, which Welch did not expect to sell unless circumstances changed. Any other businesses went outside the circles; Welch put them in three categories: "support," "ventures," and simply "outside." All were candidates for disposal – even the businesses that were supposed to support the core activities.

Balancing the portfolio

High on the list of outside operations was "housewares," the small appliance business whose toasters, kettles, and irons had played the foremost role in spreading the GE trademark around America's homes. That impressed Welch not at all. Housewares in total had the number one position in the US market: but that was not true product by product. The operation came nowhere near Welch's financial requirements and, despite vehement internal opposition, out it went.

Noel M. Tichy and Stratford Sherman comment in their book, *Control Your Destiny or Someone Else Will*, that:

> "The sale of Housewares was the first of many assaults on GEers' sentimentality that made enemies among the very people Welch meant to lead. The corporate equivalent of blasphemy became a trademark of his regime. *Although the moves were financially sound* (my italics), they hurt his public reputation."

But the idea of financial soundness was inescapable for Welch. You cannot create value for shareholders by destroying value. You dare not invest capital in businesses that do not pay. Anybody can invest unprofitably, but the task of the manager is to invest the owners' funds more wisely and successfully than they can themselves. Less exciting performers, however, have a place in achieving this goal. The rapid growth of a business like plastics might well be erratic. The dependable businesses, though, give a company "enormous staying power," in Welch's words, and underpin a balanced portfolio.

Mutual protection

Thus, Welch can approve plans for the dependables "to go from A to B," knowing how the businesses are going to make the journey, and knowing in consequence that the group as a whole will reach its planned destination. You can never be sure that a collection of businesses (or products, for that matter) will get from A to B exactly as planned. You can be certain that you have the power to complete the voyage from A to B, however much plans have to be altered:

> "If one of the businesses is going to be weak, and it's a great business, but it's in a difficult moment, I can support it. If I'm a single-product guy in a weak business like that, in a business that cycles dramatically, I get whacked. So the staying power that our businesses have allows us to stay for the long haul."

"The businesses I eliminated were not simply in the red for two or three years; they had been depressed for 30 or 50 years in the long history of GE. And their employees had consciously become underdogs."
Jack Welch Speaks

Welch systematized this approach in 1988 as the "business engine." He used the term to make it clear that, despite its diversity, GE was not a holding company whose investments operated independently. The components were parts of a larger whole, the pistons of an engine whose driver sat in the Corporate Executive Office, fueling the forward progress with human, financial, and technical resources. The businesses had to optimize their own market and financial performance by increasing productivity, allocating their resources effectively, improving their turnover of assets, and selling disposable businesses: but the earnings they generated were used for the common good.

Restructuring GE

An allied strength in a diversified business – if management is properly entrepreneurial – is the ability to pick winners that stock markets cannot see. Winners may lurk in industries that are not perceived as growth industries, but do contain growth elements. As an example, Welch cites the growth of his favorite, plastics: "We are on every PC that's being sold today, with a high-margin product. So plastics is growing." In retail lighting, the strategy was to go with the winners in distribution, like Wal-Mart, the world's largest retailer.

Portfolio structure, in Welch's philosophy, is concerned with the "hardware" of business management, which he

"The point is that you can take what seemingly look like mature industries and tie your horse to winning elements."
Control Your Destiny or Someone Else Will

distinguishes from the "software." Hardware is what you make and sell, and where you locate those operations. Software is broadly culture. The hardware inevitably comes first: operating wrong and wrongly structured businesses with improved management leads nowhere. Between 1981 and 1989 Welch took 350 product lines and business units and placed them into 13 major businesses, while many operations were eliminated in one way or another.

The $9 billion of disposals in that first decade was small in comparison to the $18 billion of acquisitions. Under Welch, GE has been a hyperactive investor. By 1998 the company had completed no fewer than 600 acquisitions. They have been swiftly and successfully integrated along the same tough lines as the original hardware restructuring of GE's existing businesses. Nobody is spared from these disciplines. In 1981–89 most of the nine layers of GE's hierarchy were removed, with 29 pay levels reduced to just five bands – and, as the total workforce fell by 100,000, profits and market value soared.

Focusing on the software

Welch was moving fast towards his goal of making GE the richest corporation, but that by no means satisfied him. Cutbacks do not create shareholder value: they reverse its waste, but creation requires positive strategies. He acted in the 1980s on concepts that were to be articulated by thinkers in the next decade, when, in a belated reaction against "downsizing" – reduction in employment by closures, sell-offs, and layoffs – observers began to notice that downsized businesses had difficulty in growing.

Cutbacks produce relatively easy, short-term payoffs. But they do not help, and may positively hinder, the generation of new business growth. Without that, Welch could not meet his targets. He saw very clearly that this was a matter of software, of the effectiveness of managers, systems, and the workforce as a whole. Creating a balanced portfolio and managing it as one entity had been achieved. "The hardware was basically in place by mid-1988," he told Tichy and Sherman in 1991. "We liked our businesses." But you also have to like the way that they are managed – and here Welch was much less happy.

Managing the agenda

Inevitably, software ideals take time to turn into reality. And Welch's next bid to raise shareholder value – "integrated diversity" – was certainly idealistic. The phrase means that businesses are run independently, but pool ideas, people, experience, best practices – everything that can improve their performance and that of the whole corporation. Work-Outs and Six Sigma (see p. 43) are essential to this very great ambition. They lead on toward a fluid, flexible, and innovative organization that can seize opportunities for long-term growth and profit.

This long-term emphasis is underpinned by a hard and unremitting emphasis on meeting short-term commitments and exercising strict cost control. A fundamental tenet of Welch's is the need to combine future results with present achievement, long-range shareholder value with immediate management results. "You can't grow long-term if you can't eat short-term," he has said. "Anybody can manage short. Anybody can manage long. Balancing these two things is what management is." His highly effective short-term action agenda is calculated to avoid anything that damages long-term performance:

- Do not add any costs.
- Speed up turnover of inventory.
- Consolidate acquisitions.
- Use intellectual capital to replace investment in plant and equipment.
- Campaign against price concessions.

The program presupposes that organizational fat has already been carved away, which was certainly true at GE. Throughout his first decade, Welch only once failed to report a quarterly rise in earnings – and that failure was down to a technical change in accounting rules. Operational earnings continued to march upward, quarter after quarter, in the next decade as well. Even though there is no evidence to show that short-term gains in earnings equate with long-term creation of shareholder value, Wall Street analysts are notoriously fixated on quarterly results.

Investor perceptions

Short-term performance therefore has a powerful effect on investor perceptions. Those have been of enormous importance in the creation of GE's corporate wealth. A string of short-term earnings, of course, translates into consistent year-by-year increases: but that is not the sole explanation for the Welch bonanza. From 1988 to 1998, earnings per share rose by 11.2 percent annually: bettered by only 87 of the 500 largest US companies. But total return to investors (meaning mostly the rise in the share price) advanced two and a half times as fast.

Part of the difference is explained by the general sustained boom on Wall Street, which had been especially marked in big corporate stocks like GE: a substantial part, however, arose from perceptions – the Welch effect. Welch made sure, via contacts with academics and the media, that the ways in which his excellent results were produced received as much publicity as the results themselves. In 1987, though, the jury was still out: "How good a manager is he?" asked one business magazine. But subsequent titles of magazine articles speak for themselves:

■ "Inside the mind of Jack Welch: GE's chairman is pushing ideas that could transform the art of management" (*Fortune*, March 27, 1989).
■ "How Jack Welch keeps the ideas coming at GE" (*Fortune*, August 12, 1991).
■ "CHAMPS! When it comes to creating shareholder wealth, these guys (Welch and the late Roberto Goizueta of Coca-Cola) are in a league of their own" (*Fortune*, December 11, 1995).
■ "How Jack Welch runs GE: a close-up look at America's No.1 manager" (*Business Week*, June 8, 1998).

Welch understands very clearly that perception is reality and has a profound effect on shareholder value. That explains some of his sensitivity to corporate wrongdoing, where GE's record is by no means free of accusations and embarrassments. That is an occupational risk of pressing hard for performance – and sometimes pressing too hard.

Adding economic value

Pressure for performance is one way in which the concept of creating wealth for the shareholders is translated into the life of the manager down the line. It is not the most important method, however. If managers can be persuaded to think like owners, their work is much more likely to benefit the latter. Welch strives to achieve this identification. Much of his approach is in tune with the idea of Economic Value Added (or EVA). The basic, simple notion is that the company should earn more on its capital than the capital employed actually costs – which means that individual managers must do the same.

What lent wings to this age-old principle in the 1990s was the redefinition of capital to include equity. If you look at the cost of the dividend alone, equity is usually much cheaper than debt. But equity shareholders expect a higher total return on their investments than debtholders: with that premium expectation added in, equity capital is more expensive than debt. The return that must be achieved on capital, once the latter has been defined in this way, is also substantially higher. The targets are stretched – as Welch insists that they must be.

Less outlay, more return

Reducing total capital employed while increasing its productivity sums up the basic thrust of Welch's wealth creation. Meeting his targets demands that managers cut down the total capital they need (by reducing inventories, for example) while increasing the efficiency with which it is used (for instance, by getting more productivity from the machines). If the individual managers meet their targets, so must the company. The emphasis shifts heavily to the efficient management of resources and getting a bigger bang per buck.

Although Welch did not specifically use EVA, the results of following this general philosophy were just what its advocates would predict. In 1995, GE's cost of capital was calculated by *Fortune* magazine at 12.9 percent. Its return on that capital was 14.8 percent. That added up to an excess of $863 million, which the stock market multiplied an amazing number of times. Market Value Added, or MVA, basically calculates all the capital that a company has accumulated over time and compares that sum with the current stock market value of the equity and debt.

The ultimate endorsement

For 1994, that calculation gave GE an MVA of $52 billion, nearly all of it added during Welch's reign. The MVA went on increasing over the rest of a decade in which GE's and Welch's reputations continued to soar. There were still dissenting voices, however. In 1997, the German magazine *Der Spiegel* called Welch "The Brutal Manager" and pointed out, in an interview with the GE boss, that: "As the number of employees was halved, the share price increased almost twentyfold." Then it asked Welch whether shareholder value was more important to him than the families of his former employees. His answer was "No":

"In a global economy, you cannot manage a company in a paternalistic way just because it feels better. If you don't sort things out in good time they will eventually explode in your face. Then you have to become brutal and cruel."

Welch's approach, at any rate, has received the highest possible endorsement at home. In February 2000, *Fortune* magazine reported that Welch's peers among America's 500 top executives had voted GE the country's most admired company for the third year running. It won by its all-around achievement on the list of eight attributes of admirable performance; they included innovativeness, employee talent, financial soundness, use of corporate assets, long-term investment value, social responsibility, and quality of products and/or services.

The rating vindicates Welch's simple-sounding theory that you create the right value by taking the right actions, right across the organization and all its activities. The great manager enriches the owners (and thus himself) by investing in the right businesses, exiting from the wrong ones, pressing and incentivizing business leaders for optimum performance, and launching powerful initiatives to sustain momentum and exploit the forces of change. And in these tasks, the leader never rests.

Ideas into action

- Make managers set their own stretch targets and ensure that these are met.

- Balance fast-growth, higher-risk businesses with dependable and steady ones.

- Eat short-term if you want to grow long-term – concentrate on the present as well as the future.

- Educate managers to think like owners, and give them sound incentives to do so.

- Make sure that you like both your businesses and how they are managed.

- Reduce total capital employed while raising its productivity.

- See that employees are enriched along with the outside investors.

5

Exploiting the forces of change

How the internet creates immense new business opportunities ● Why reaching the top is a beginning, not a culmination ● **How Welch discovered a potential crisis behind GE's bulging order books** ● The way to force through change in a company that is apparently successful ● **Reaching down into the organization to inspire everybody** ● The way to govern strategy by latching onto a single strong idea ● **Boundarylessness** ● Living by the three themes of reality, quality/ excellence, and the human element

Jack Welch's entire career at the summit of General Electric is testimony to a truth in which he strongly believes. He argues that becoming Chief Executive Officer is not, as many CEOs have thought, the culmination of a career: it is a beginning. His own predecessors at GE acted in the same belief. The tradition is that each incoming CEO takes a fresh look at the corporation's position, external and internal, and ordains the changes that changing times make mandatory.

Welch saw clearly that he had taken command at a watershed. The hyperinflation of the 1970s had coincided with threats from the East, primarily from Japan, where poor quality and low price had been succeeded by a deadly combination of high quality and low price. GE was in the firing line in many of its businesses. There was no option: GE's plants, quality, and discipline had to change to achieve the level reached by competitors overseas.

Facing the competition

Welch has never hesitated to express the truth as he sees it. In October 1981, 120 leading executives were given a blunt ultimatum. The issue for his audience, the new CEO told them, was having to face reality about troubled situations. That was not a difficulty for Welch and his top team at the Fairfield, Connecticut, headquarters:

"We can take good news and we can take bad news. We're big people and we've been paid well, all of us. You own these damn businesses. The idea of coming into Fairfield, and Fairfield yells, and Big Daddy gets you – it's an insane system we've built. No, you are the owners of your businesses. For God's sake, take them and run with them. Get us out of the act."

Welch wanted the business leaders to examine their situation in 1981, then look at the likely position in 1985 and ("probably more important") 1990. Could they participate in those arenas as the number one or number two player? This meant tremendous change along three dimensions. Welch wanted to establish a wholly new contract between Fairfield and the businesses. He wanted their leaders to take full responsibility, not just for their financial results, but for the totality of their management. And any businesses that could not pass the one-or-two test would be axed or radically changed, one way or another.

The problem Welch faced was one that defeated a contemporary CEO at IBM, John Akers, who once told a similar group of senior managers that "everyone is too comfortable when the business is in crisis!" In IBM's case, the crisis (which went uncured) was already apparent in falling market shares. But GE's problems were hidden by a gigantic backlog of orders. Welch is brilliant at looking behind the figures. He could see that the $28 billion orderbook that he had inherited was a snare and a delusion.

Losing battler
While GE was steered clear of the competitive threat by Welch, IBM, then headed by John Akers (below), never succeeded in reclaiming its former dominant position in computer hardware.

As GE went on delivering power stations, turbines, and locomotives – all products with long lead-times, ordered in the previous decade – the revenues and profits would roll in during the 1980s, however badly current sales were doing. To the managers he was trying to change, however, the backlog was a comfortable cushion. All they could see was the corporation's good overall performance: they could not relate Welch's diatribe to a financial year in which profits had risen 9 percent to some $1.7 billion.

The challenge of change

Change (the biggest challenge, according to Welch) is always easier to propose than to achieve, even for an exceptionally vigorous manager. Welch was accused of going too far, too fast. He has often said, though, that his mistake was not in moving too fast, but too slowly. He makes a distinction between evolutionary change and revolution. Welch is widely perceived by outsiders (and no doubt insiders also) as revolutionary. Yet he thinks that: "We didn't get at these things fast enough. It took us a decade to do a lot of the things we had to do."

In presenting the challenge of change to his people, Welch does not pretend to be a prophet. He works on general feelings about the dominant trends of the times. His reading of the trends is based on observation and personal experience. For example, he reckoned in the late 1990s that "my job is three times as fast as it was." Compared to 1980, in his view, the activity and pace in the CEO's role make it hardly even the same game.

One crucial factor in this continuing acceleration is that "information's going to be everywhere." Typically, Welch reacted more rapidly than most leaders of established companies to the advent of the internet. GE led the way in setting up a corporationwide website through which the purchase of goods and services could be centralized, with potential savings in the billions. As a supplier, you either tendered via the website, or you waved goodbye to GE.

But Welch realizes that the internet is a sea change. Its threat and opportunity go far deeper than improvement, however rewarding, in existing processes. What about the brand new? Long before the dot.com companies were born, established competitors had almost universally shown themselves incapable of resisting the challenge of new disruptive technologies – of which the net is an extreme example. Any GE business, Welch reckoned, might be disrupted by someone who had a new way of serving customers that left GE behind. His reaction was pure Welch: disrupt yourself rather than be disrupted.

Destroyyourbusiness.com

In 1999, he ordered every division to select an e-commerce leader: they were to launch "destroyyourbusiness.com," an operation that would seek to pre-empt disruptive moves by outsiders. The e-leaders placed in charge of the dot.com attackers had to be well versed in the internet and possess disruptive temperaments. Welch was determined to see GE win a large share of the e-commerce pie, and he used "e-briefs" on the internet to make his intentions clear.

"I don't know what the world's going to be; all I know is it's going to be nothing like it is today. It's going to be faster."
Control Your Destiny or Someone Else Will

For all his awareness of the internet problem, Welch declared that the destroyers would not be rewarded with separate equity linked to their dot.com ventures. This meant that GE risked losing the brightest and best to start-ups that could make them multimillionaires overnight. Having succeeded so long (and so greatly) with integrated diversity, Welch was deeply unwilling to disintegrate his creation. He was prepared to reward people for performance, but the team came first: in Welch's GE even the top 30 Corporate Executive Council members would not last long "if they're not team players."

The ultimate resolution of this particular dilemma, however, must rest with his successor. In 2000, his last year, Welch simply lacked the time to demonstrate that GE, unlike many past giants, could win the competitive wars with a new, disruptive technology or marketing approach. To some extent, GE could learn to win by acquisition. For instance, in 1999 the company bought xoom.com, a direct marketing website of phenomenal growth (616 percent in a single year) that was fed into NBC and without question brought with it a wholly different culture.

No central strategy

How would such injections affect the immensely strong culture of GE? The enormous impact of the world wide web, with the first website opened as late as 1993, amply confirms two of Welch's main tenets. First, change is not predictable. Second, it cannot be controlled. These two governing ideas, which reflect Welch's lifetime in a highly diversified corporation, have led him to take a wholly pragmatic approach to cultural change and corporate strategy – which must go hand in hand.

As early as December 1981, he told a business audience that "We have all learned... that it is impossible to forecast with any precision," and that "It just doesn't make sense for neatness' sake to shoehorn these initiatives into an all-inclusive, all-GE central strategy." Rather, Welch put his faith in "a central idea – a simple core concept that will guide General Electric... and govern our diverse plans and strategies." He thought that in the slow-growth environment of the 1980s, the winners would insist on being "the number one or number two leanest, lowest cost, worldwide producers of quality and services or those who have a clear technological edge, a clear advantage in a market niche." He cited business guru Peter Drucker's famous "very tough question:"

"'If you weren't already in the business, would you enter it today?' And if the answer is no... (there is) a second difficult question: 'What are you going to do about it?'"

United responses to change

Welch has enormous respect for Drucker, whom he has often consulted: but his favorite management writer, significantly enough, is a soldier – Helmuth von Moltke, once military adviser to the Ottoman Empire. Von Moltke argued that "strategy was not a lengthy action plan, but rather the evolution of a central idea through continually changing circumstances." Being number one or number two was a tangible central idea: but Welch surrounded it with intangible central values, "unifying dominant themes that, because of GE's common culture, will become second nature in the organization." In the face of change, Welch proposed that GE should embrace three specific themes:

- Reality: getting the organization and the groups of people within it to see the world the way it is, and not as they would wish or hope to see it.
- Quality/excellence: creating an atmosphere where every individual in the organization strives to be proud of every product and service that it provides.
- The human element: creating an innovative atmosphere where people are confident that how far and how fast they move is constrained only by the limits of their creativity and drive and by their standards of personal excellence.

But there is a fourth, equally important theme: Welch's belief that these "soft values" truly can become "second nature in the organization." To him, it is feasible to "permeate every mind in this company." He talks elsewhere (see p. 49) of "changing the fundamental DNA of the company." In fact, GE's own experience under this most enthusiastic of management hot gospelers – who has often expressed disappointment with the limited degree to which minds in GE have been permeated – demonstrates that cultural change has important limits.

Educating the organization

Limits to cultural change are established by differences in individual makeup and by different interactions among individuals in groups. This kaleidoscopic pattern changes over time, but usually the change is slow. The pattern was severely and sharply disturbed by Welch:

"For a long time our actions muddied communications. We were taking out lots of people. We were taking out layers of management. We were selling off businesses. We were impacting people's lives."

As that passage indicates, Welch may be a hyperactive leader but he is not a hyperactive change manager. Rather, he recognizes that one of the greatest mistakes in change management is to pursue too many initiatives for too short a time — initiatives that are very often abandoned well before the objectives are achieved. "If you have an idea *du jour*," he says, "you're dead."

The role of leaders is to drive home the themes that matter, to expand the reach of their communication, refine it, get better at it. In GE's case, says Welch:

"... it began to snowball. If you have a simple, consistent message, and you keep on repeating it, eventually that's what happens. Simplicity, consistency, and repetition — that's how you get through. It's a steady continuum that finally reaches a critical mass."

Boundarylessness

The final theme of Welch's reign, a preoccupation that grew more and more insistent over the 1990s, was "boundarylessness" — a "big, big idea." Hard to describe, and harder still to put into action, the boundaryless ideal arises when somebody "knows where I stand. I know where he stands. We don't always agree — but we trust each other." Welch hammers home the need for an open, trusting sharing of ideas, a willingness to listen and debate, and a determination to take the best ideas and act on them. As Noel M. Tichy and Stratford Sherman reported in *Control Your Destiny or Someone Else Will*, Welch said in 1992: "If this company is to achieve its goals, we've all got to become boundaryless. Boundaries are crazy."

He regards trades unions, with whom his relations, often uneasy, have nevertheless been productive, as just another boundary. Managers have to reach across that boundary, just as they need to reach across the boundaries separating them from customers and suppliers, and from colleagues overseas and at home. With boundarylessness, as with his other key ideas, Welch embarked on a long road of indoctrination:

"… we've got to keep repeating it, reinforcing it, rewarding it, living it, letting everybody know all the time that when they're doing things right, it's because their behavior is boundaryless."

It is unlikely that the ideal of boundarylessness became second nature inside GE by the end of 2000. The difficulty is that drawing bounds, and refusing to cross them, is also natural. Top management thus has an additional educational role – and, in fact, Welch's GE has often been praised as a true "learning company," an organization that builds collective and individual knowledge.

The thinking company

Welch places equal emphasis, though, on the "thinking company," whose capital is ideas and which exploits these intellectual assets by debate and by change. He seeks "the antithesis of blind obedience." Within a context of strong financial and other disciplines, people must develop enough self-confidence to express opposing views. get all

"Companies need overarching themes to create change. If it's just somebody pushing a gimmick or a program, without an overarching theme, you can't get through the wall."
Control Your Destiny or Someone Else Will

the facts on the table, and respect differing opinions. "It is our preferred mode of learning; it's how we form balanced judgements. We value the participation, involvement, and conviction this approach breeds."

The acme of the thinking, changing company is seen at the sessions in "The Pit," the large amphitheater at Crotonville. Welch thinks that people feel comfortable in this setting: "Everyone's close together. The people asking questions are looking down at the speaker. Somehow that opens up the questioning." That helps to establish the facts. Welch believes that bright people, when confronted with the same facts, in an atmosphere of openness and candor, will come up with the same answers:

"This may not be true in religion and philosophy and a lot of other things, but in business you're dealing with a fairly quantitative process. It's concrete. It's simple. This is not rocket scientist work. If we all have the same information, we'll all come to roughly the same conclusions."

Faster responses

As the 1980s ended, however, Welch was feeling increasingly frustrated. No matter how hard he pressed the case for openness, candor, and change, they were not being achieved in the businesses. He needed these and other attributes to achieve his growth targets. Flying back by helicopter from GE's Crotonville management center in September 1988, Welch discussed this software issue with its then director, James Baughman. How could the open exchange of ideas at Crotonville be transferred into the businesses? A week later Baughman came up with an answer: Work-Out (see p. 43). In January 1989 — four

Architect of Work-Out
James Baughman, as director of Crotonville, designed the Work-Out procedure for Welch, providing a means by which employees could suggest ways to improve working processes and practices.

months after the chopper trip – the 500 top operating managers learned that the plan was already being enacted.

Fast responses are critical to Welch's philosophy. He notes that many businesses wait to act and tolerate long lead-times – not just for product development, but for corporate change. Managements often allow trading to deteriorate for years before trying to institute reform. They may pay lip service to change, but in reality they fear and distrust a process that by definition threatens the status quo and their managerial control. Welch has this to say:

"The old organization was built on control, but the world has changed. The world is moving at such a pace that control has become a limitation. It slows you down. You've got to balance freedom with some control, but you've got to have more freedom than you ever dreamed of."

His genius lies not only in recognizing this truth, but in forcing through radical changes when GE was riding high, when the case for change was in his mind, rather than in the marketplace or in the minds of his managers.

Ideas into action

- Make business managers lead by taking total responsibility for their units.

- To change people's mind-sets, first seek to change their results.

- See the internet challenge through the eyes of a hungry competitor.

- Ask, "If I was not in the business already, would I enter it today?" If not, leave.

- Introduce the soft values that you want and make them become second nature in the organization.

- Never fall into the trap of having a constantly changing "idea *du jour.*"

- Press for a faster speed of response as the key to competitive advantage.

Breaking bounds

Welch's bid to make GE a boundaryless organization itself has no frontiers. Whether a boundary is inside or outside the company, it limits performance. Individuals unwittingly set their own bounds, limiting what they achieve. Challenge all barriers and seek to tear them down. And set stretch targets for your company and for yourself.

Examining the boundaries

When Welch took over GE, the company structure included nine layers of management, from the CEO to the shop floor, each forming a boundary. Welch took out whole layers, but delayering affects only vertical boundaries: there are two other types.

The Three Types of Boundary		
1 Vertical	**2 Horizontal**	**3 External**
The hierarchical steps that separate different layers of management.	The barriers between different functions, departments, country units, operating units.	The frontiers between the business and its suppliers, customers, and competitors.

Breaking down internal barriers

The fewer internal borders there are to cross, the better for the overall efficiency of your company. Tackle vertical and horizontal barriers by implementing the following practices:

- Scrap inhibitions about crossing a layer – encourage managers to talk to the subordinates of other managers, and *vice versa*.
- Use development programs and task forces to mix different vertical levels in a nonhierarchical setting.
- Use cross-functional, interdepartmental teams to break down horizontal boundaries.
- Ask people who interrelate with other areas of the company to provide assessments of the service they receive; link rewards to the ratings given.
- Mingle purposefully, positively, and often.
- Encourage people to visit others from whom they can learn.

JACK WELCH

Breaking down external barriers

The most dramatic moves towards boundarylessness are external, and not confined to the inner workings of a company. To optimize your business you must optimize the whole business system by bringing in the key outsiders: suppliers and customers.

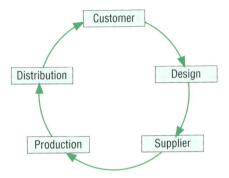

The business system

Remove barriers and strengthen links between each element in the business system to achieve improved company performance and greater satisfaction.

Strengthening links

Encourage the fall of barriers between the company and the outside world. Go to see customers and find out what improvements you can make for their benefit, and implement findings wherever possible. Work with suppliers to reform the business system to achieve shared gains. Form alliances, even with competitors, to take advantage of any complementary strengths. Then take the following systematic steps with your new "allies":

- Customers: involve in product development, encourage self-service, and obtain and act on feedback.
- Distributors: integrate with supply, and turn into inventory holder – even subcontractor.
- Producers: link production to outside suppliers, distributors, and customers; make to order.
- Suppliers (external): link to production/distribution, supplying daily, just in time.
- Design staff: involve suppliers and customers, to build in value, quality, and superior performance.

Ask yourself: "Am I helping my colleagues, customers, and suppliers to get the best from me?" and "Am I working to get the best from them?" Make sure you get the right answers.

1 Stretching other people

What you measure in management generally governs what you get. So if you set goals below the capability of a person or an organization, underperformance is likely to result. Transcend the aims that people believe feasible, and the opposite may well happen.

Establishing realistic targets

Jack Welch's concept of stretch starts with producing realistic targets – for profitability, for instance, or new product introductions. Such targets must pass the following three criteria:

- They are "do-able."
- They are reasonable.
- They are within the organization's or individual's capabilities.

Set your own targets for your part of the business, making sure they fulfill these three criteria. These realistic targets are indispensable since they enable you to set a baseline, to authorize expenditure, and to apply comparisons that help to monitor trends and spotlight problem areas.

Setting stretch targets

Now take your realistic targets and attach a much higher goal – a stretch target – to each one. These goals may "at the outset seem to require superhuman efforts to achieve," says Welch, but "by reaching for what appears to be impossible, we often actually do the impossible; and even when we don't quite make it, we inevitably wind up doing much better than we would have done."

Achieving the Impossible

Welch imposed on one of his managers a daunting stretch target to improve productivity: the impossible-seeming goal was achieved in four years.

When Jack Welch found that rival makers of CT-scanners and X-ray machines were getting 50,000 scans per tube, against GE's 25,000, he demanded a quadrupling of tube life. Confronted with this "impossible" target, the division eventually accomplished the superhuman. Tubes finally appeared that lasted for 150,000–200,000 scans. The new methods required also provided other very valuable benefits.

JACK WELCH

Work out your stretch targets every bit as carefully as your realistic targets. If, for example, your stretch target is to double the budgeted level of sales, ask yourself:

■ What does that imply for revenue per salesperson, per customer, and per product?

■ What are the consequences for production and distribution – can the commitment be met?

Searching out sin

Without high aims, you will not achieve extraordinary results. Most companies are all too satisfied with run-of-the-mill performance, complacent in the assumption that their achievement is superior. One of Welch's greatest lessons is that success always conceals failure. However good the organization is, it is certain to be guilty of many sins – of omission and commission.

Left unconfessed and uncured, these sins can undermine the strongest companies. The only safe course is to be your own Grand Inquisitor, constantly probing for points of weakness and setting new stretch targets. If you can cut costs, raise productivity, and sharpen competitive edge when business is good, the payoff is far greater than if you wait for bad results to stimulate action.

Do not make the inquisition negative. Challenge your company with six key questions that will raise everyone's sights and encourage people to become positive inquisitors themselves.

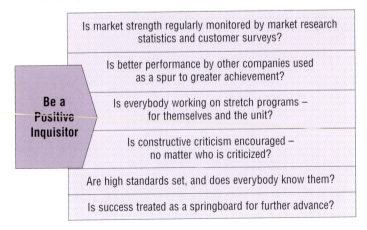

Be a Positive Inquisitor
Is market strength regularly monitored by market research statistics and customer surveys?
Is better performance by other companies used as a spur to greater achievement?
Is everybody working on stretch programs – for themselves and the unit?
Is constructive criticism encouraged – no matter who is criticized?
Are high standards set, and does everybody know them?
Is success treated as a springboard for further advance?

2 Stretching yourself

Apply the concept of stretch to your own career and you will find that, as with company stretch targets, the higher you aim, the more you are likely to achieve. Back up your lofty aims with ambitious self-development to ensure complete success.

Reaching the summit

When Jack Welch named his personal objective – to be Chief Executive of GE – eight years of effort lay ahead before he reached the top. He was still the youngest CEO in the company's history. Study the steps of his 21-year climb listed below and write down your own hoped-for progression. How high do you want to go? What time must you allow? What preparations must you make?

Jack Welch's Road to the Top	
Years with firm	**Progress to the summit**
+21	Chief executive (run whole organization)
+19	Challenge for top (named vice-chairman)
+17	Head several businesses (run business sector)
+13	Get corporate position (run business group)
+8	General manager (run plastics business)
+3	Take charge (head chemical development)
+0	Use expertise (develop plastics)
0	Learn expertise (chemical engineering)

Developing motivation

You may not share Welch's level of ambition. Few people do. But most people operate with a view of their potential that significantly limits that potential.

Every manager knows cases of failed and fired employees who, transferred to another business, have far exceeded their previous performance. The explanation is not only that they moved from a demotivating environment to one where their talent was given a real chance. Their personal motivation was also spurred by the impact of dismissal and the need to make good in a new job. Develop that motivation in yourself by reaching for the skies.

Aiming high

Do not be satisfied with the best you can do now and the best you think you can do. Be bold, like Welch, and strike out for the highest promotions and achievements that may be within your reach. Appoint yourself as your own career manager, and approach the task as you would an important project for the organization.

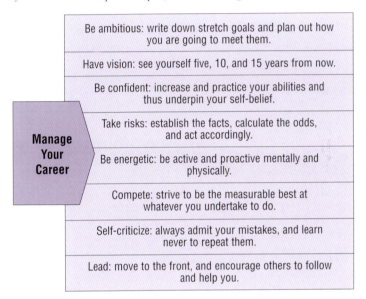

Manage Your Career

Be ambitious: write down stretch goals and plan out how you are going to meet them.
Have vision: see yourself five, 10, and 15 years from now.
Be confident: increase and practice your abilities and thus underpin your self-belief.
Take risks: establish the facts, calculate the odds, and act accordingly.
Be energetic: be active and proactive mentally and physically.
Compete: strive to be the measurable best at whatever you undertake to do.
Self-criticize: always admit your mistakes, and learn never to repeat them.
Lead: move to the front, and encourage others to follow and help you.

Looking ahead

Taking the long view in your career will concentrate your mind on what you need to do in preparation for the next promotion. It is a test of your self-confidence. Nobody will have confidence in you unless you have confidence in yourself.

As a relative junior, Welch would introduce his requests for capital with an account of his successful use of previous allocations. That is not bragging. It is being objective about what you can do or have done. The young Welch also took the initiative energetically, taking the lead in seizing his plastics opportunities.

You will not always win the competition, or always be the best. But if you do not try, losing will become a self-fulfilling prophecy. Welch made his own and his company's luck. You can do the same.

GLOSSARY

BEST PRACTICE: Top-of-the-class methods and ideas for every aspect of business, transferable between companies and company units.

BOUNDARYLESSNESS: Removal of barriers between people, departments, and businesses – and the outside agencies with which they deal.

BUSINESS ENGINE: GE metaphor for a company driven by interaction between its various component parts (or "pistons").

CEC: Corporate Executive Council, comprising the top 30 officers of GE, which meets every quarter at CROTONVILLE.

CORE: Businesses that are intended to be long-term corporate holdings and are not for sale.

CROTONVILLE: Site of GE's management institute in Croton-on-Hudson, NY.

E-BRIEFS: Messages used to stimulate GE management to take full advantage of internet opportunities.

FAIRFIELD: Connecticut site of GE corporate headquarters.

EVA: Economic Value Added – the difference between the cost of all capital and the profit made on capital.

GROCERY STORE: Welch's affectionate nickname for GE.

HARD, AND HARDWARE: Measurable processes and results, and the physical assets required for them (*see also* SOFT, AND SOFTWARE).

INTEGRATED DIVERSITY: Concept of GE as a diverse collection of businesses that provide mutual support and learn from each other.

"MOST ADMIRED COMPANY": Accolade in *Fortune* magazine, won by GE for three years running.

MVA: Market Value Added – the difference between the capital invested by a company and its quoted market value.

NEUTRON JACK: Nickname (after the neutron bomb that exterminates all life, leaving buildings intact) given to Jack Welch during his massive program of layoffs in the 1980s.

P&L RESPONSIBILITY: Accountability for the financial results (Profit & Loss) of a unit.

PROCESS MAPPING: Procedure of describing and analyzing a business process from beginning to end with a view to streamlining the process.

SESSION C: Annual GE meetings at which the CEO discusses all managers and their future with operating heads.

SHAREHOLDER VALUE: The worth of the company to its owners, which is generally equated with the market value of its equity.

SIX SIGMA: Much-prized standard of quality performance in which no more than 3.4 defects per million parts or operations are acceptable.

SOFT, AND SOFTWARE: Management processes that are not measurable but which generate "hard" results (*see also* HARD, AND HARDWARE).

SPAN OF CONTROL: The number of people directly managed or controlled by one person.

THE PIT: Large auditorium at CROTONVILLE where management debates, conferences, and presentations are staged.

VALUES: Written principles that are agreed companywide and are intended to govern behavior and produce lasting success for the subscribing corporation.

WORK-OUT: Innovatory, three-day, offsite meetings at which employees debate procedure and efficiency issues, suggesting solutions that management evaluates at the end of the third day.

BIBLIOGRAPHY

Even if Jack Welch continues to resist any temptation to write his own account of his life, time, and theories, there will be no shortage of words about this most extraordinary of business leaders. Over his two decades as CEO of General Electric, Welch has given innumerable interviews, delivered many public speeches, and left nobody in any doubt about what he thinks and why he has acted as he did. *Jack Welch Speaks*, by Janet C. Lowe, draws extensively on this material and gives an excellent account of the key events in its subject's life and his most important ideas.

The author who has been closest to Welch, however, is Noel M. Tichy, a professor at the University of Michigan and a former director of Crotonville, GE's management training center in Croton-on-Hudson. The establishment is very dear to Welch's heart, and has served as the centerpiece of his drive to instill new thinking into GE's managers at all levels. Tichy and his co-author, Stratford Sherman, provide a valuable "Handbook for Revolutionaries" among many key "Lessons for Mastering Change" – which is the subtitle of their book about Welch. Its main title, *Control Your Destiny or Someone Else Will*, is a maxim that Welch learned at his mother's knee, and is a fundamental of his management philosophy.

In *The GE Way Fieldbook*, by former *Time* journalist Robert Slater, there is much highly practical advice in "modules" that cover leadership, empowerment, organization, and customers; the book also looks at Welch as professor, communicator, and strategist. Slater has written no fewer than three other books on Welch – *The New GE: How Jack Welch Revived an American Institution* (McGraw Hill, 1992); *Get Better or Get Beaten* (Irwin Professional, 1994), which offers 31 of Welch's "Leadership Secrets"; and *Jack Welch and the GE Way*.

Most of the Welch literature is laudatory – which is not surprising, given his brilliant record. Thomas F. O'Boyle does strike a more critical note in *At Any Cost: Jack Welch and the Pursuit of Profit* (Random House, 1998). But his quarrel appears to be more with American corporate capitalism in general than with any real wrongdoing by its most spectacular practitioner.

WORKS CITED

Janet C. Lowe (1998) *Jack Welch Speaks*, John Wiley & Sons, Inc., New York
Robert Slater (1998) *Jack Welch and the GE Way*, McGraw-Hill, New York
– (2000) *The GE Way Fieldbook*, McGraw-Hill, New York
Noel M. Tichy and Stratford Sherman (1993) *Control Your Destiny or
    Someone Else Will*, HarperCollins Publishers Inc., New York

Index

Page numbers in *italics* refer to picture captions.

JACK WELCH

Robert Heller

Robert Heller is himself a prolific author of management books. The first, *The Naked Manager*, published in 1972, established Heller as an iconoclastic, wide-ranging guide to managerial excellence – and incompetence. Heller has drawn on the extensive knowledge of managers and management he acquired as the founding editor of *Management Today*, Britain's premier business magazine, which he headed for 25 years. Books such as *The Supermanagers* and *In Search of European Excellence* address the ways in which the latest ideas on change, quality, and motivation are providing new routes to business success. In 1990 Heller wrote *Culture Shock*, one of the first books to describe how IT would revolutionize management. Since then, as writer, lecturer, and consultant, Heller has continued to tell managers how to "Ride the Revolution," the title of his 2000 book, written with Paul Spenley. His books for Dorling Kindersley's Essential Managers series are international bestsellers.